Betty Crocker's

SENSATIONAL SALADS

Macmillan • USA

MACMILLAN
A Simon and Schuster Macmillan Company
15 Columbus Circle
New York, NY 10023

Library of Congress Cataloging-in-Publication Data
Crocker, Betty.
    Betty Crocker's sensational salads.
        p.   cm.
    Includes index.
    ISBN 0-02-860280-3
    1. Salads. 2. Menus.   I. Title.   II. Title: Sensational salads.
    TX740.C686   1995
    641.8'3—dc20   94-36647
            CIP

Manufactured in the United States of America
10 9 8 7 6 5 4 3 2 1

First Edition

Front Cover: Greek Pasta Salad (page 46), Whole Wheat Fettucine with Spring Vegetables (page 48)

Back Cover: Salmon Salad with Cucumber Noodles (page 74)

Contents

—■—

Introduction

◼

Salads are increasing in popularity because they are healthful, easy and perfect for so many different types of meals. You have full creative license when making a salad, from main-dish salads for lunch or dinner to fruit and vegetable salads as accompaniments to any meal. With their color, zest and versatility, salads are welcome anytime—at buffet suppers, casual picnics, elegant luncheons, or family meals. They are perfect for dinner on a hectic work day or on a hot summer day when you don't want to spend a lot of time in the kitchen. Convenience products make salads even easier with grocers now selling meats and vegetables already "salad friendly," cut up and ready to go.

We have gathered the best salad recipes here, ones that showcase their ease and diversity. In the mood for a meat salad? You can choose from a classic like Chef's Salad, or try something more unusual like Asian Beef Salad, Southwestern Pork Salad or Broiled Sirloin and Mushroom Salad. Looking for a salad with poultry? Toss up Chicken Pasta Salad, Crunchy Chicken and Pear Salad or Curried Turkey and Rice! Thinking about fish or shellfish? Marinated Shrimp Kabob Salad, Crab Louis or Fresh Tuna and Red Potato Salad are sure to please. In addition, we have included an entire chapter on meatless salads and one dedicated to fruit and vegetable salads containing such delicacies as Lentil and Wild Rice Salad, Vegetable Couscous Salad, or Mexicali Pasta Salad plus classics like Potato Salad, Cole Slaw and Fresh Fruit Salad.

We have also included a useful chart to help you make colorful, appetizing tossed salad, plus lots of practical hints on seasoning, storing and serving your salads. With so many delicious salads to choose from, whether you are looking for main-dish, side-dish or just great taste, you'll find just what you want in BETTY CROCKER'S SENSATIONAL SALADS.

THE BETTY CROCKER EDITORS

Salad Savvy

GREENS BASICS

Choosing salad greens is often the first step in creating a tossed salad or main-dish salad. Knowing the different types of greens available lets you make inventive and satisfying salads.

- Crisphead (or iceberg) lettuce has a mild flavor that makes it the most popular green. Look for solid, compact heads with tight leaves that range from medium-green outer leaves to pale green inside.
- Boston (or butterhead) lettuce has a small, rounded head of soft buttery-feeling leaves that have a delicate flavor.
- Bibb (or limestone) lettuce has tender, pliable leaves similar to those of Boston. Bibb is smaller than Boston but has a similar delicate, mild flavor.
- Romaine (or cos) has narrow, elongated dark leaves with a crisp texture.
- Leaf lettuce—red, bronze or green—has tender leaves that don't form heads. These leafy bunches have a mild, though sometimes nutty, flavor.
- Belgian or French endive has closed, narrow, pale leaves with a pleasantly bitter flavor.
- Curly endive has frilly, narrow leaves with a slightly bitter flavor.

- Escarole, also part of the endive family, is a less frilly, broad-leafed endive with dark green leaves.
- Radicchio, another member of the endive family, resembles a small loose-leaf cabbage with smooth, tender leaves. The Rosso variety has rose-colored leaves with white veins, and Castelfranco, blander and sweeter, has leaves sprinkled with pink, green and red flecks or swirls.
- Watercress has rounded dark green leaves on leggy stems, with a strong, peppery flavor.
- Arugula (or rocket) has small, slender leaves with a rich, bitter flavor. Choose smaller leaves for less assertive flavor.
- Spinach has smooth, tapered, dark green leaves, sometimes crumpled at the edges.
- Sorrel, also known as sourgrass, looks similar to spinach but its leaves are smaller. Sorrel has a sharp, lemony flavor.

- Cabbage comes in a variety of types. Green and red cabbage are the most familiar. Look for compact heads. Savory Cabbage has crinkled leaves and Chinese (or Napa) cabbage has long, crisp leaves.

SELECTING AND STORING SALAD GREENS

- Be sure greens are fresh when purchased. Avoid limp or bruised greens and greens with rust spots.
- Store greens in the crisper of the refrigerator in the original wrapping or place in a plastic bag until needed. Wash them when ready to use.
- Be sure to wash greens thoroughly in several changes of cold water. For greens that may be sandy, such as spinach, separate leaves with fingers to remove all grit. Gently blot dry to remove remaining moisture; refrigerate.
- Watercress, parsley and fresh herbs should be refrigerated in screwtop jars filled with water. Make sure stems are in the water.
- Romaine and iceberg lettuce will keep nicely in the refrigerator up to a week. Most other greens wilt within a few days of purchasing.
- If you plan to use iceberg lettuce within a day or two, remove the core before washing. Strike the core end against a flat surface; then twist and lift out the core. Hold the head, core end up, under running water to separate and clean leaves. Turn right side up and drain thoroughly. Refrigerate in a plastic bag or bowl with an airtight lid.

SERVING SALAD GREENS

- Use a variety of greens for complementary textures, flavors and colors. And remember, fresh herbs can perk up even the simplest combinations.
- Mix dark greens with light, crisp with tender, and straight with curly. Red leaf (bronze) lettuce provides both color and delicate flavor. Red cabbage and radicchio also add color and texture.
- Blot any leftover moisture you find in leaf crevices; the drier the leaves, the better. Tear, don't cut, greens into bite-size pieces. Pour dressing on just before serving, using only enough to coat the leaves lightly; then toss. Or serve the salad with dressing on the side so that each person can add the desired amount.

HOW TO USE NUTRITION INFORMATION

Nutrition information per serving for each recipe includes the amounts of calories, protein, carbohydrate, fat cholesterol and sodium.

- If ingredient choices are given, the first listed ingredient is used in recipe nutrition information calculations.
- When ingredient ranges or more than one serving size is indicated, the first weight or serving is used to calculate nutrition information.
- "If desired" ingredients and recipe variations are not included in nutrition information calculations.

Tossed Salad Chart

(serves 4 to 6)
Mix all ingredients in a large salad bowl and toss with your favorite dressing.

Salad Greens	Salad Additions	Garnish With
Choose one or more to total 5 cups	*Choose one or more to total 1 cup*	*Choose one or more to total 1/4 to 1/3 cup*
Arugula	Alfalfa sprouts	Cheese
Bibb lettuce	Asparagus	Bacon, crisply cooked, crumbled
Boston lettuce	Broccoli flowerets	Croutons
Cabbage	Bell peppers	Eggs, hard-cooked
Endive	Carrots	Edible flowers
Escarole	Cauliflowerets	French-fried onions
Iceberg lettuce	Cucumbers	Fresh herbs
Leaf lettuce	Mushrooms	Nuts
Radicchio	Onions	Olives
Romaine	Peas	Sunflower nuts
Spinach	Radishes	Toasted wheat germ
Watercress	Tomatoes	
	Zucchini	
	Fruit	
	Meat, poultry or fish, cooked	

Herbs, Seeds and Spices in Salads

Herbs and spices are nature's gifts to the good salad maker. Used discriminately, they enhance rather than overwhelm with their flavors and fragrances.

Name and Type	Flavor	Form(s)	Kind of Salad
Basil (herb)	sweet, clovelike	dried leaves, ground	tossed
Cayenne pepper (spice)	hot, peppery	ground	main dish
Celery seed	slightly bitter	whole, ground	fruit, vegetable
Chili powder	spicy, hot	ground	vegetable
Chives (herb)	less harsh than onion	freeze-dried	vegetable
Cinnamon	aromatic, pungent	stick, ground	fruit
Cloves (spice)	aromatic, pungent	whole, ground	fruit
Cumin (aromatic seed)	savory, slightly bitter	whole, ground	tossed, vegetable
Curry powder	pungent, hot to mild	ground	vegetable
Dill weed (herb)	pungent	whole, dried	tossed
Garlic (dehydrated)	pungent aroma and taste	minced, powdered	tossed, vegetable main dish
Ginger (spice)	pungent, spicy	whole, cracked (bits), ground	fruit, vegetable
Marjoram (herb)	aromatic, slightly sweet	dried leaves, ground	tossed, vegetable, main dish
Mint (herb)	strong, sweet, cool aftertaste	dried leaves, flakes	fruit, tossed, vegetable, main dish
Mustard (aromatic seed)	hot, pungent, dry aftertaste	whole seed, ground	main dish
Nutmeg (spice)	fragrant, sweet, spicy	whole, ground	fruit
Oregano (herb)	strong, aromatic, pleasantly bitter	dried leaves, ground	main dish
Paprika (spice)	sweet to hot	ground	main dish
Parsley (herb)	slightly peppery	fresh, dried leaves	fruit, tossed, vegetable, main dish
Tarragon (herb)	piquant, similar to anise	dried leaves	tossed
Thyme (herb)	aromatic, pungent	dried leaves, ground	tossed
Turmeric (spice)	aromatic, slightly bitter	ground	main dish

Menus

Quick Mid-Week Salad
Tangy Steak Salad (page 34)
Garlic Bread
Brownies or Cookies
Milk

Light and Easy Lunch
Chef's Salad (page 41)
Pita Bread
Lemon Sorbet or Frozen Yogurt
Iced Tea

South-of-the-Border Supper
Layered Mexican Salad (page 57)
Salsa and Guacamole with Tortilla Chips
Fajita Salad (page 33)
Vanilla Pudding with Fresh Mango
Beer or Milk

Warming Wintertime Dinner
Hot Chicken Salad with Plum Sauce (page 16)
Vegetable Soup
Whole Wheat Bread
Blueberry Cobbler
Herbal Tea or Warm Apple Cider

Perfect Picnicking Fare
Summer Garden Beef Salad (page 29)
Gazpacho Pasta Salad (page 49)
Rolls and Butter
Easy Fruit Salad (page 93)
Wine or Fruit Juice

Elegant Entertaining
Grilled Salmon Salad (page 70)
Wilted Mixed Greens Salad (page 86)
Baked Red-skin Potato
Breadsticks
Chocolate Swirl Cheesecake
Coffee or Tea

International Dinner
German-style Hot Chicken Salad (page 18)
French Potato Salad (page 83)
String Beans
Crusty French Bread
Fruit Tarts
Seltzer with Fruit Juice

Chicken-Pasta Salad

1
Poultry Salads

Chicken-Pasta Salad

You'll love this quick salad on a busy night!

1 package (6 ounces) frozen pea pods
1 package (5 ounces) spiral macaroni
¹/₃ cup mayonnaise or salad dressing
¹/₄ cup French dressing
2 cups cut-up cooked chicken (about 12 ounces)
1 cup cherry tomatoes, cut into halves

Remove pea pods from package. Place pea pods in bowl of cool water until thawed; drain. Cook macaroni as directed on package—except add pea pods about 2 minutes before macaroni is done; drain. Rinse macaroni and pea pods with cold water; drain. Mix mayonnaise and French dressing in large bowl. Add macaroni mixture and remaining ingredients; toss. **4 servings**

SERVING SIZE: 1 Serving 480 Calories (235 Calories from Fat); Fat 26 g (Saturated 5 g); Cholesterol 80 mg; Sodium 380 mg; Carbohydrate 36 g; (Dietary Fiber 2 g); Protein 27 g; *% Daily Value:* Vitamin A 4%; Vitamin C 46%; Calcium 4%; Iron 20%

Hot Curried Chicken Salad

2 cups cut-up cooked chicken or turkey
³/₄ cup mayonnaise or salad dressing
2 tablespoons finely chopped onion
2 tablespoons capers, drained
1 teaspoon curry powder
¹/₂ teaspoon salt
4 stalks celery, thinly sliced
¹/₂ cup toasted slivered almonds

Heat oven to 350°. Mix all ingredients except almonds. Spoon into ungreased 1-quart casserole or six 1-cup baking dishes. Sprinkle with almonds.

Bake uncovered until chicken mixture is hot, about 20 minutes. **6 servings**

SERVING SIZE: 1 Serving 365 Calories (290 Calories from Fat); Fat 32 g (Saturated 5 g); Cholesterol 55 mg; Sodium 400 mg; Carbohydrate 4 g; (Dietary Fiber 2 g); Protein 17 g; *% Daily Value:* Vitamin A 2%; Vitamin C 2%; Calcium 4%; Iron 10%

Chicken-Vermicelli Salad

We've kept the fat low and the flavor high in this fresh chicken salad.

8 ounces uncooked vermicelli
Ginger Dressing (below)
2 cups cut-up cooked chicken or turkey
1¹/₂ cups shredded carrots
1 cup coarsely chopped cucumber
¹/₂ cup coarsely chopped jicama or water chestnuts
¹/₄ cup chopped fresh cilantro or parsley

Break vermicelli into halves. Cook vermicelli as directed on package—except omit salt; drain. Rinse with cold water; drain. Prepare Ginger Dressing in large bowl. Add vermicelli and remaining ingredients; toss. Spoon onto salad greens, if desired.   **6 servings**

Ginger Dressing

¹/₃ cup cholesterol-free reduced-calorie mayonnaise or salad dressing
¹/₃ cup plain nonfat yogurt
1 tablespoon reduced-sodium soy sauce
1 teaspoon sugar
¹/₂ teaspoon ground ginger
Dash red pepper sauce

Mix all ingredients.

SERVING SIZE: 1 Serving 305 Calories (70 Calories from Fat); Fat 8 g (Saturated 2 g); Cholesterol 40 mg; Sodium 380 mg; Carbohydrate 38 g; (Dietary Fiber 2 g); Protein 20 g; % *Daily Value:* Vitamin A 38%; Vitamin C 16%; Calcium 6%; Iron 14%

Raspberry Chicken Salad

Use any raspberries you like, so long as they are unsweetened. Fresh black and golden are the more unusual alternatives to red.

4 cups bite-size pieces mixed salad greens (iceberg, Bibb, romaine or spinach)
2 cups cut-up cooked chicken
1 cup raspberries*
¹/₃ cup thinly sliced celery
¹/₄ cup toasted sliced almonds
Raspberry Dressing (below)
Freshly ground pepper

Toss salad greens, chicken, raspberries and celery; sprinkle with sliced almonds. Serve with Raspberry Dressing and pepper.   **4 servings, about 1³/₄ cups salad and ¹/₃ cup dressing each**

Raspberry Dressing

1 cup plain nonfat yogurt
¹/₂ cup raspberries*
1 tablespoon raspberry or red wine vinegar
2 teaspoons sugar

Place all ingredients in blender container. Cover and blend on high until smooth, about 15 seconds.

*Frozen unsweetened loose-pack raspberries can be substituted for the fresh raspberries.

SERVING SIZE: 1 Serving 250 Calories (90 Calories from Fat); Fat 10 g (Saturated 2 g); Cholesterol 60 mg; Sodium 115 mg; Carbohydrate 16 g; (Dietary Fiber 3 g); Protein 27 g; % *Daily Value:* Vitamin A 2%; Vitamin C 24%; Calcium 18%; Iron 12%

Chicken and Plum Salad

Fennel Seed Dressing (below)
4 skinless, boneless chicken breast
halves (about 1 pound)
2 teaspoons vegetable oil
4 plums, sliced
1 cup sliced celery (about 2 medium
stalks)
2 cups small cauliflowerets
Lettuce leaves or bite-size pieces lettuce

Prepare Fennel Seed Dressing. Cook chicken breast halves in oil in 10-inch nonstick skillet about 6 minutes on each side or until juices run clear. Cool slightly; cut into thin slices. Toss plums, celery, cauliflowerets and dressing in large bowl. Carefully stir in chicken. Cover and refrigerate at least 4 hours. Spoon onto lettuce leaves. **6 servings**

Fennel Seed Dressing

$1/4$ **cup dry white wine or apple juice**
2 tablespoons vegetable oil
1 teaspoon fennel seed
1 teaspoon sugar
1 teaspoon chopped fresh or $1/4$ teaspoon
dried rosemary leaves
1 teaspoon chopped fresh or $1/4$ teaspoon
dried tarragon leaves
$1/2$ **teaspoon salt**
Dash of ground red pepper (cayenne)

Shake all ingredients in tightly covered container.

SERVING SIZE: 1 Serving 190 Calories (80 Calories from Fat); Fat 9 g (Saturated 2 g); Cholesterol 45 mg; Sodium 240 mg; Carbohydrate 9 g; (Dietary Fiber 2 g); Protein 18 g; *% Daily Value:* Vitamin A 4%; Vitamin C 26%; Calcium 2%; Iron 6%

Yields for Cooked Poultry

Cook more chicken or turkey than you need and have a supply for recipes using leftovers of each. You can expect about 3 to 4 cups cooked meat from a 3- to 4-pound broiler-fryer chicken; 10 to 12 cups meat from a 6- to 6-pound rolled turkey roast, and 14 cups from a 12-pound turkey.

An easy way to cook turkey is poaching. Cut turkey into quarters and place in a large kettle with enough water to cover the bottom of the kettle. Sprinkle with 2 tablespoons of salt and 2 teaspoons of white pepper. Heat to boiling. Reduce heat and cover and simmer until turkey is done, 2 to $2^1/_2$ hours. Remove turkey quarters from broth and refrigerate for at least 1 hour but no longer than 2 days. Remove the meat from the bones and cut up.

Crunchy Chicken and Pear Salad

Lemon-Mayonnaise Dressing (below)
3 cups cubed cooked chicken or turkey
2 cups chopped firm pears (about
   2 medium)
3/4 cup sliced red onion (about 1 small)
3/4 cup chopped celery (about 1 large stalk)
3/4 cup chopped mushrooms (about
   3 ounces)
1/2 cup chopped green onions (about
   5 medium)
2 tablespoons chopped fresh or
   2 teaspoons dried tarragon leaves
Lettuce leaves

Prepare Lemon-Mayonnaise Dressing in large bowl. Add remaining ingredients except lettuce leaves; toss. Cover and refrigerate at least 1 hour. Serve on lettuce leaves.   **6 servings**

Lemon-Mayonnaise Dressing

1/2 cup plain nonfat yogurt
2 tablespoons cholesterol-free reduced-
   calorie mayonnaise or salad dressing
2 teaspoons grated lemon peel
2 tablespoons lemon juice
1 tablespoon rice vinegar or white wine
   vinegar
1 tablespoon Dijon mustard
1/2 teaspoon salt
1/4 teaspoon pepper

Mix all ingredients in a glass or plastic bowl.

SERVING SIZE: 1 Serving 200 Calories (45 Calories from Fat); Fat 5 g (Saturated 1 g); Cholesterol 55 mg; Sodium 320 mg; Carbohydrate 15 g; (Dietary Fiber 3 g); Protein 24 g; % Daily Value: Vitamin A 4%; Vitamin C 18%; Calcium 8%; Iron 8%

Chicken and Orange Salad

2 tablespoons finely chopped scallions or
   green onions (with tops)
2 tablespoons lime juice
1/4 teaspoon salt
2 cups cut-up cooked chicken
1 cup cooked green peas
1 cup mayonnaise or salad dressing
1/4 cup finely chopped carrot
1/4 cup finely chopped celery
1/4 cup finely snipped fresh cilantro
3 tablespoons orange juice
1/2 teaspoon salt
1/2 teaspoon ground cinnamon
1/4 teaspoon freshly ground pepper
Lettuce leaves
3 oranges, peeled and sectioned or
   unpeeled and cut into wedges
2 avocados, peeled and cut into wedges

Sprinkle scallions with lime juice and 1/4 teaspoon salt; cover and refrigerate. Mix remaining ingredients except lettuce, oranges and avocados; cover and refrigerate at least 1 hour.

Spoon chicken mixture onto lettuce. Garnish with oranges and avocados; sprinkle with scallions.   **6 servings**

SERVING SIZE: 1 Serving 490 Calories (370 Calories from Fat); Fat 41 g (Saturated 7 g); Cholesterol 60 mg; Sodium 550 mg; Carbohydrate 19 g; (Dietary Fiber 6 g); Protein 17 g; % Daily Value: Vitamin A 20%; Vitamin C 84%; Calcium 6%; Iron 12%

Chicken-Rice Salad

Ginger-Lemon Dressing (below)
3 cups cut-up cooked chicken or turkey
2 cups cold cooked rice
2 cups cut-up fresh pineapple or 1 can (20 ounces) pineapple chunks in juice, drained
$1/3$ cup chopped celery (about 1 medium stalk)
$1/2$ cup shredded carrot (about 1 medium)
$1/4$ cup chopped onion (about 1 small)
Lettuce leaves
1 cup alfalfa sprouts
2 tablespoons salted sunflower nuts

Prepare Ginger-Lemon Dressing. Mix chicken, rice, pineapple, celery, carrot and onion; toss with Ginger-Lemon Dressing. Cover and refrigerate until cold, at least 4 hours. Serve on lettuce leaves; top with alfalfa sprouts. Sprinkle with sunflower nuts.   **6 servings (about 1 cup)**

Ginger-Lemon Dressing

$1/3$ cup vegetable oil
3 tablespoons lemon juice
1 tablespoon honey
$1/4$ to $1/2$ teaspoon ground ginger
$1/8$ teaspoon garlic powder
4 to 6 drops red pepper sauce

Shake all ingredients in tightly covered jar.

SERVING SIZE: 1 Serving 360 Calories (160 Calories from Fat); Fat 18 g (Saturated 4 g); Cholesterol 60 mg; Sodium 70 mg; Carbohydrate 28 g; (Dietary Fiber 2 g); Protein 24 g; *% Daily Value:* Vitamin A 22%; Vitamin C 26%; Calcium 4%; Iron 14%

Chicken and Fruit Salad with Green Chili Dressing

Vary the heat of this dressing by using either mild or hot chilies—whatever suits your taste.

3 cups bite-size pieces salad greens and shredded red cabbage
2 cups cut-up cooked chicken or turkey
$1 1/2$ pounds honeydew, cantaloupe, casaba or Spanish melon, cut into thin wedges
2 cups bite-size pieces pineapple (about $1/2$ medium)
$1/2$ small jicama, cut into julienne strips, or 2 stalks celery, sliced
Green Chili Dressing (below)

Arrange salad greens and cabbage on platter or 4 salad plates; top with chicken, melon, pineapple and jicama. Garnish with lime slices and cilantro sprigs, if desired. Serve with Green Chili Dressing.   **4 servings**

Green Chili Dressing

1 cup mayonnaise or salad dressing
2 tablespoons lime juice
1 to 2 tablespoons finely chopped mild or hot green chilies
1 green onion (with top), thinly sliced, or 2 tablespoons snipped cilantro

Mix all ingredients.

SERVING SIZE: 1 Serving 630 Calories (440 Calories from Fat); Fat 49 g (Saturated 8 g); Cholesterol 90 mg; Sodium 390 mg; Carbohydrate 26 g; (Dietary Fiber 3g); Protein 24 g; *% Daily Value:* Vitamin A 30%; Vitamin C 100%; Calcium 6%; Iron 14%

Oriental Chicken Salad

Cellophane noodles are hard, clear noodles made from mung peas. They become white, puffy and crisp when deep-fried, puffing up to more than twice their original size. Remove them quickly from the oil so that they stay white.

Ginger Dressing (below)
Vegetable oil
1 package (3³/₄ ounces) cellophane noodles (bean threads)*
¹/₂ head lettuce, shredded (about 4 cups)
3 cups cut-up cooked chicken or turkey
1 medium carrot, shredded (about ¹/₂ cup)
4 green onions (with tops), sliced (about ¹/₄ cup)
1 tablespoon sesame seed, toasted

Prepare Ginger Dressing. Heat oil (1 inch) in Dutch oven to 425°. Fry ¹/₄ of the noodles at a time about 5 seconds, turning once, until puffed; drain.

Pour Ginger Dressing over lettuce, chicken, carrot and onions in large bowl. Toss with half the noodles. Place remaining noodles on large platter. Spoon salad over noodles. Sprinkle with sesame seed.   **6 servings**

Ginger Dressing

¹/₃ cup vegetable oil
¹/₄ cup white wine vinegar
1 tablespoon sugar
2 teaspoons soy sauce
¹/₂ teaspoon pepper
¹/₂ teaspoon ground ginger
¹/₄ teaspoon salt

Shake all ingredients in tightly covered container. Refrigerate at least 2 hours.

*5 cups chow mein noodles can be substituted for the fried cellophane noodles. Toss half the noodles with chicken-dressing mixture. Continue as directed.

SERVING SIZE: 1 Serving 340 Calories (225 Calories from Fat); Fat 25 g (Saturated 4 g); Cholesterol 60 mg; Sodium 270 mg; Carbohydrate 8 g; (Dietary Fiber 1 g); Protein 22 g; *% Daily Value:* Vitamin A 20%; Vitamin C 8%; Calcium 4%; Iron 10%

Hot Chicken Salad with Plum Sauce

2 teaspoons olive or vegetable oil
4 skinless boneless chicken breast halves (about 1 pound)
1 can (16 ounces) purple plums in juice, rinsed, drained and pitted
1 tablespoon lemon juice
2 teaspoons packed brown sugar
¹/₄ teaspoon ground ginger
¹/₈ teaspoon crushed red pepper
1 clove garlic
4 cups shredded Chinese cabbage
1 cup bean sprouts (about 2 ounces)
1 tablespoon thinly sliced green onion with top (about ¹/₂ medium)

Heat oil in 10-inch nonstick skillet over medium heat. Cook chicken breast halves, turning once, about 10 minutes or until done.

Place remaining ingredients except cabbage, bean sprouts and onion in blender or food processor. Cover and blend on high speed or process about 30 seconds or until smooth. Heat sauce, if desired.

Arrange cabbage, bean sprouts and onion on 4 serving plates. Top with chicken. Spoon plum sauce over chicken.   **4 servings**

SERVING SIZE: 1 Serving 240 Calories (65 Calories from Fat); Fat 7 g (Saturated 2 g); Cholesterol 65 mg; Sodium 110 mg; Carbohydrate 17 g; (Dietary Fiber 3 g); Protein 30 g; *% Daily Value:* Vitamin A 24%; Vitamin C 72%; Calcium 10%; Iron 12%

Chili-Chicken Salad

Salad Dressing (below)
3 cups cut-up cooked chicken or turkey
2 tablespoons finely chopped onion
$1/4$ teaspoon salt
1 can (4 ounces) chopped green chilies,
    drained
6 cups bite-size pieces lettuce (about
    1 medium head)
2 medium tomatoes, cut into thin wedges

Prepare Salad Dressing. Mix chicken, onion, salt, chilies and Salad Dressing in large bowl. Add lettuce and tomatoes; toss.

8 servings

Salad Dressing

$1/4$ cup vinegar
2 tablespoons sugar
2 tablespoons vegetable oil
$1/2$ teaspoon salt
$1/2$ teaspoon ground cumin

Shake all ingredients in tightly covered container.

SERVING SIZE: 1 Serving 150 Calories (65 Calories from Fat); Fat 7 g (Saturated 2 g); Cholesterol 45 mg; Sodium 410 mg; Carbohydrate 6 g; (Dietary Fiber 0 g); Protein 16 g; % Daily Value: Vitamin A 2%; Vitamin C 26%; Calcium 2%; Iron 6%

Mexican Chicken Salad

2 cups cut-up cooked chicken
$1/4$ cup sour cream
$1/4$ cup mayonnaise or salad dressing
$1/4$ cup finely chopped carrot
2 tablespoons snipped fresh cilantro
2 tablespoons capers
2 tablespoons chopped pimiento
2 tablespoons lime juice
$1/2$ teaspoon ground cumin
$1/2$ teaspoon dried oregano leaves
1 small onion, chopped (about $1/4$ cup)
Lettuce leaves
1 avocado, peeled and cut into wedges
Paprika

Toss all ingredients except lettuce, avocado and paprika. Serve on lettuce with avocado; sprinkle with paprika.

4 servings

SERVING SIZE: 1 Serving 335 Calories (225 Calories from Fat); Fat 25 g (Saturated 6 g); Cholesterol 75 mg; Sodium 150 mg; Carbohydrate 8 g; (Dietary Fiber 3 g); Protein 22 g; % Daily Value: Vitamin A 24%; Vitamin C 26%; Calcium 4%; Iron 12%

Southern Chicken Salad

Peaches and pecans add a southern flavor to this chicken salad.

**4 skinless boneless chicken breast halves
  (about 1 pound)
1 cup dry white wine or chicken broth
Buttermilk Dressing (below)
2 medium stalks celery, finely chopped
  (about 1 cup)
3 medium peaches, coarsely chopped, or
  1 package (16 ounces) frozen sliced
  peaches, thawed and chopped
1 head Boston lettuce, torn into bite-size
  pieces
1 cup chopped pecans, toasted**

Place chicken breast halves in 10-inch skillet; pour wine into skillet. Cook over medium heat 10 to 15 minutes, turning once, until juices of chicken run clear; drain. Cool chicken. Prepare Buttermilk Dressing.

Cut chicken into 1-inch pieces. Mix chicken, celery and peaches in large bowl. Add 1/4 cup of the dressing; toss to coat. Cover and refrigerate 1 hour. Arrange lettuce on large serving plate. Spoon chicken mixture onto lettuce. Sprinkle with pecans. Serve with remaining dressing.

6 servings

Buttermilk Dressing

**1/2 cup mayonnaise or salad dressing
1/2 cup buttermilk
2 tablespoons chopped fresh or
  2 teaspoons dried tarragon leaves
1/2 teaspoon salt**

Shake all ingredients in tightly covered container.

SERVING SIZE: 1 Serving 385 Calories (270 Calories from Fat); Fat 30 g (Saturated 3 g); Cholesterol 50 mg; Sodium 370 mg; Carbohydrate 12 g; (Dietary Fiber 2 g); Protein 19 g; *% Daily Value:* Vitamin A 6%; Vitamin C 10%; Calcium 6%; Iron 10%

German-style Hot Chicken Salad

**4 boneless skinless chicken breast halves
  (about 1 pound)
1/4 cup vegetable oil
1 tablespoon all-purpose flour
1/4 cup water
2 tablespoons white wine vinegar
2 teaspoons Dijon-style mustard
1 tablespoon snipped fresh thyme leaves
  or 1 teaspoon dried thyme leaves
2 ounces mushrooms, sliced (about
  3/4 cup)
2 green onions (with tops), thinly sliced
Salt and pepper to taste
1/2 bunch romaine, torn into bite-size
  pieces
2 medium tomatoes, cut into wedges**

Cook chicken breast halves in oil in 10-inch skillet over medium heat until done, about 6 minutes on each side. Remove chicken from skillet. Drain; cool slightly. Cut into thin slices.

Stir flour into drippings in skillet. Cook over low heat, stirring constantly, until smooth and bubbly. Remove from heat; stir in water, vinegar, mustard, thyme, mushrooms and onions. Cook over low heat, stirring constantly, until mixture is bubbly. Cook and stir 1 minute. Sprinkle with salt and pepper.

Divide romaine among 4 salad plates. Arrange chicken and tomatoes on romaine; spoon mushroom mixture over top **4 servings**

SERVING SIZE: 1 Serving 290 Calories (155 Calories from Fat); Fat 17 g (Saturated 3 g); Cholesterol 65 mg; Sodium 370 mg; Carbohydrate 7 g; (Dietary Fiber 1 g); Protein 28 g; *% Daily Value:* Vitamin A 16%; Vitamin C 20%; Calcium 40%; Iron 14%

German-style Hot Chicken Salad

Cobb Salad

Lemon Vinaigrette (below)
6 cups finely shredded lettuce
2 cups cut-up cooked chicken
3 hard-cooked eggs, chopped
2 medium tomatoes, chopped (about
    1 1/2 cups)
1 ripe avocado, chopped
1/4 cup crumbled blue cheese (1 ounce)
4 slices bacon, crisply cooked and
    crumbled

Prepare Lemon Vinaigrette. Divide lettuce among 4 salad plates or bowls. Arrange remaining ingredients in rows on lettuce. Serve with Lemon Vinaigrette.   **4 servings**

Lemon Vinaigrette

1/2 cup vegetable oil
1/4 cup lemon juice
1 tablespoon red wine vinegar
2 teaspoons sugar
1/2 teaspoon salt
1/2 teaspoon dry mustard
1/2 teaspoon Worcestershire sauce
1/4 teaspoon garlic powder
1/4 teaspoon pepper

Shake all ingredients in tightly covered container. Refrigerate at least 1 hour.

SERVING SIZE: 1 Serving 590 Calories (430 Calories from Fat); Fat 48 g (Saturated 10 g); Cholesterol 230 mg; Sodium 600 mg; Carbohydrate 12 g; (Dietary Fiber 3 g); Protein 31 g; % Daily Value: Vitamin A 16%; Vitamin C 40%; Calcium 10%; Iron 16%

Chicken Salad Filling

Make your favorite sandwich with these versatile sandwich fillings!

1 1/2 cups chopped cooked chicken or
    turkey
1/2 cup mayonnaise or salad dressing
1 medium stalk celery, chopped (about
    1/2 cup)
1 small onion, chopped (about 1/4 cup)
1/4 teaspoon salt
1/4 teaspoon pepper

Mix all ingredients.   **about 2 cups filling
(enough for 4 sandwiches)**

SERVING SIZE: 1 Serving 300 Calories (225 Calories from Fat); Fat 25 g (Saturated 5 g); Cholesterol 60 mg; Sodium 340 mg; Carbohydrate 3 g; (Dietary Fiber 0 g); Protein 16 g; % Daily Value: Vitamin A 2%; Vitamin C 2%; Calcium 2%; Iron 6%

BEEF SALAD FILLING: Substitute 1 1/2 cups chopped cooked beef for the chicken. Stir in 2 tablespoons sweet pickle relish, drained.

EGG SALAD FILLING: Substitute 6 hard-cooked eggs, chopped, for the chicken.

HAM SALAD FILLING: Substitute 1 1/2 cups chopped fully cooked smoked ham for the chicken. Omit salt and pepper. Stir in 1 teaspoon prepared mustard.

TUNA SALAD FILLING: Substitute 1 can (9 1/4 ounces) tuna in water, drained, for the chicken. Stir in 1 teaspoon lemon juice.

Turkey-Macaroni Salad

1¹/₂ **cups uncooked elbow or spiral**
 macaroni (about 6 ounces)
1 package (10 ounces) frozen green peas
2 cups cut-up cooked turkey or chicken
³/₄ **cup cholesterol-free reduced-calorie**
 mayonnaise or salad dressing
¹/₂ **cup shredded reduced-fat Cheddar**
 cheese
¹/₂ **cup sliced green onions (about**
 5 medium)
¹/₂ **cup sliced celery (about 1 medium**
 stalk)
¹/₃ **cup sweet pickle relish**
3 cups bite-size pieces lettuce (about
 ¹/₂ **medium head)**

Cook macaroni as directed on package—except omit salt; drain. Rinse with cold water; drain. Rinse frozen peas with cold water to separate; drain. Mix macaroni, peas and remaining ingredients except lettuce. Cover and refrigerate about 4 hours or until chilled. Serve on lettuce.

6 servings

SERVING SIZE: 1 Serving 375 Calories (135 Calories from Fat); Fat 15 g (Saturated 4 g); Cholesterol 45 mg; Sodium 500 mg; Carbohydrate 37 g; (Dietary Fiber 4 g); Protein 23 g; % Daily Value: Vitamin A 6%; Vitamin C 14%; Calcium 10%; Iron 16%

Fruited Turkey Salad

3 cups cut-up cooked turkey or chicken
³/₄ **cup seedless grape halves**
2 medium stalks celery, thinly sliced
 (about 1 cup)
2 green onions (with tops), thinly sliced
1 can (11 ounces) mandarin orange
 segments, drained
1 can (8 ounces) sliced water chestnuts,
 drained
1 carton (6 ounces) lemon, peach or
 orange yogurt (about ²/₃ **cup)**
2 tablespoons soy sauce

Mix turkey, grapes, celery, onions, orange segments and water chestnuts. Mix yogurt and soy sauce. Pour over turkey mixture and toss. Cover and refrigerate at least 2 hours.

6 servings, about 1¹/₄ cups each

SERVING SIZE: 1 Serving 215 Calories (45 Calories from Fat); Fat 5 g (Saturated 2 g); Cholesterol 60 mg; Sodium 430 mg; Carbohydrate 21 g; (Dietary Fiber 1 g); Protein 23 g; % Daily Value: Vitamin A *%; Vitamin C 24%; Calcium 8%; Iron 8%

Curried Turkey and Rice Salad

¹/₂ **cup cholesterol-free reduced-calorie**
 mayonnaise or salad dressing
¹/₂ **cup plain nonfat yogurt**
³/₄ **teaspoon curry powder**
¹/₂ **teaspoon ground ginger**
¹/₄ **teaspoon salt**
¹/₄ **teaspoon ground red pepper (cayenne)**
3 cups cold cooked rice
2 cups cut-up cooked turkey or chicken
1 cup sliced celery (about 2 medium
 stalks)
¹/₂ **cup chopped bell pepper (about 1 small)**
1 can (15¹/₄ ounces) pineapple chunks in
 juice, drained
Salad greens
2 medium tomatoes, cut into wedges

Mix mayonnaise, yogurt, curry powder, ginger, salt and red pepper in large glass or plastic bowl. Stir in rice, turkey, celery, bell pepper and pineapple. Cover and refrigerate about 2 hours or until chilled. Just before serving, line 6 salad plates with salad greens. Divide salad evenly among plates. Garnish with tomato wedges.

6 servings

SERVING SIZE: 1 Serving 340 Calories (90 Calories from Fat); Fat 10 g (Saturated 2 g); Cholesterol 40 mg; Sodium 660 mg; Carbohydrate 45 g; (Dietary Fiber 3 g); Protein 18 g; % Daily Value: Vitamin A 4%; Vitamin C 38%; Calcium 8%; Iron 14%

Turkey and Apricot Salad

Turkey and Apricot Salad

2 cups cut-up cooked turkey or chicken
1/2 cup Coconut-Orange Dressing (below)
1 cup julienne jicama or 1 can (8 ounces)
sliced water chestnuts, drained
1 package (6 ounces) dried apricots
2 large oranges, sectioned
2 medium carrots, coarsely shredded

Toss all ingredients. Cover and refrigerate until chilled, about 1 hour. Spoon onto salad greens, if desired. **4 servings**

Coconut-Orange Dressing

1 can (9 ounces) cream of coconut
2 teaspoons grated orange peel
1/2 cup vegetable oil
1/4 cup orange juice
1/2 teaspoon salt
1/4 teaspoon curry powder

Stir all ingredients until thick. Cover and refrigerate until ready to serve. Stir before serving.

NOTE: Remaining dressing can be used for fruit salads or as a dip for fruit.

SERVING SIZE: 1 Serving 680 Calories (405 Calories from Fat); Fat 45 g (Saturated 17 g); Cholesterol 60 mg; Sodium 350 mg; Carbohydrate 51 g; (Dietary Fiber 7 g); Protein 25 g; % *Daily Value:* Vitamin A 88%; Vitamin C 100%; Calcium 10%; Iron 30%

Turkey-Pesto Salad

This lower-fat pesto is a delicious variation of the standard pesto.

Pesto (below)
2 cups cut-up cooked turkey or chicken
3/4 cup chopped tomato (about 1 medium)
2 tablespoons sliced green onions
1 can (8 ounces) sliced water chestnuts, drained
4 cups shredded Bibb lettuce
2 tablespoons crumbled feta cheese

Prepare Pesto. Mix turkey, tomato, onions and water chestnuts. Serve on lettuce. Spoon Pesto over salad. Sprinkle with cheese. **4 servings**

Pesto

3/4 cup firmly packed fresh basil leaves
1/4 cup grated Parmesan cheese
1 tablespoon pine nuts
2 tablespoons olive or vegetable oil
1 tablespoon plain nonfat yogurt
1 tablespoon lemon juice
2 cloves garlic

Place all ingredients in blender or food processor. Cover and blend on medium speed about 2 minutes, stopping occasionally to scrape sides, until almost smooth.

SERVING SIZE: 1 Serving 300 Calories (135 Calories from Fat); Fat 15 g (Saturated 4 g); Cholesterol 65 mg; Sodium 210 mg; Carbohydrate 15 g; (Dietary Fiber 3 g); Protein 26 g; % *Daily Value:* Vitamin A 8%; Vitamin C 27%; Calcium 22%; Iron 20%

Turkey Taco Salad

Ordinary taco salads run about 200 calories higher per serving than this slimmed down version. Although an 8-inch flour tortilla has 130 calories, take a hint from the tortilla strips below and stretch them.

3 flour tortillas (8-inch)
1/2 pound ground turkey
1/3 cup water
1 to 2 teaspoons chili powder
1/2 teaspoon salt
1/4 teaspoon garlic powder
1/4 teaspoon ground red pepper
1 can (8 ounces) kidney beans, drained
5 cups shredded lettuce
1 cup chopped tomato (about 1 medium)
1/2 cup shredded Monterey Jack cheese (2 ounces)
1/4 cup chopped onion (about 1 small)
1/4 cup reduced-calorie Thousand Island dressing
1/4 cup reduced-calorie sour cream
4 pitted ripe olives, sliced

Heat oven to 400°. Cut tortillas into 12 wedges, or strips about 3 × 1/4 inch. Place in ungreased jelly roll pan, 15 1/2 × 10 1/2 × 1 inch. Bake, stirring at least once, until golden brown and crisp, 6 to 8 minutes; cool.

Cook and stir ground turkey in 10-inch nonstick skillet over medium heat until brown. Stir in water, chili powder, salt, garlic powder, red pepper and kidney beans. Heat to boiling; reduce heat. Simmer uncovered, stirring occasionally, until liquid is absorbed, 2 to 3 minutes; cool 10 minutes.

Mix lettuce, tomato, cheese and onion in large bowl; toss with Thousand Island dressing. Divide among 4 serving plates; top each salad with about 1/2 cup turkey mixture. Arrange tortilla wedges around salad. Garnish with sour cream and ripe olives.

4 servings, about 1 3/4 cups each

SERVING SIZE: 1 Serving 350 Calories (145 Calories from Fat); Fat 16 g (Saturated 6 g); Cholesterol 60 mg; Sodium 920 mg; Carbohydrate 34 g; (Dietary Fiber 4 g); Protein 22 g; *% Daily Value:* Vitamin A 16%; Vitamin C 16%; Calcium 20%; Iron 20%

Turkey Salad with Honey Almonds

Creamy Honey Dressing (below)
1/2 cup honey-roasted almonds
8 ounces thinly sliced cooked turkey or chicken, cut into 1/4-inch strips (about 2 cups)
4 ounces provolone or Swiss cheese, cut into cubes
2 medium stalks celery, sliced
2 unpeeled tart red apples, cut into cubes
Salad greens

Prepare Creamy Honey Dressing. Toss dressing and remaining ingredients except salad greens. Spoon onto salad greens; sprinkle with additional honey-roasted almonds, if desired.

4 servings

Creamy Honey Dressing

1/2 cup sour cream or plain yogurt
2 tablespoons honey
1 tablespoon snipped parsley or 1 teaspoon parsley flakes
1 teaspoon dry mustard
1 to 2 teaspoons lemon juice

Mix all ingredients in large bowl.

SERVING SIZE: 1 Serving 475 Calories (260 Calories from Fat); Fat 29 g (Saturated 11 g); Cholesterol 90 mg; Sodium 500 mg; Carbohydrate 28 g; (Dietary Fiber 4 g); Protein 29 g; *% Daily Value:* Vitamin A 16%; Vitamin C 18%; Calcium 30%; Iron 14%

Turkey Salad with Honey Almonds

Wild Rice and Turkey Salad

½ cup mayonnaise or salad dressing
¼ cup chutney
1 to 1½ teaspoons curry powder
½ teaspoon salt
3 cups cold cooked wild rice*
2 cups cut-up cooked turkey or chicken
2 cups broccoli flowerets

Mix mayonnaise, chutney, curry powder and salt in large bowl. Add wild rice, turkey and broccoli; toss. Cover and refrigerate at least 1 hour.

4 servings

*1 package (6¼ ounces) long grain and wild rice, prepared as directed on package and refrigerated until cold, can be substituted for the wild rice.

SERVING SIZE: 1 Serving 485 Calories (245 Calories from Fat); Fat 27 g (Saturated 5 g); Cholesterol 75 mg; Sodium 500 mg; Carbohydrate 35 g; (Dietary Fiber 2 g); Protein 27 g; % Daily Value: Vitamin A 8%; Vitamin C 70%; Calcium 4%; Iron 14%

Turkey–Green Bean Salad

3 cups cubed cooked turkey or chicken
3 cups 1-inch pieces cooked green beans
   (about 1 pound)
1 cup sliced jicama (about ½ medium)
1 cup plain nonfat yogurt
¼ cup chopped fresh cilantro leaves
⅓ cup lemon juice
2 tablespoons frozen (thawed) apple juice
   concentrate
½ teaspoon salt
¼ teaspoon pepper
3 cups chopped lettuce (about ½ medium
   head)

Mix all ingredients except lettuce in large glass or plastic bowl. Cover and refrigerate at least 1 hour. Serve on lettuce.

6 servings

SERVING SIZE: 1 Serving 180 Calories (25 Calories from Fat); Fat 3 g (Saturated 1 g); Cholesterol 55 mg; Sodium 280 mg; Carbohydrate 13 g; (Dietary Fiber 3 g); Protein 25 g; % Daily Value: Vitamin A 6%; Vitamin C 30%; Calcium 14%; Iron 10%

Speedy Salad Ideas

- Main-dish salads are terrific for weeknight meals because they can be assembled so quickly. Convenience products help you to have dinner ready when you are.
- Purchase prewashed, packaged lettuce combinations. Many types are available, from iceberg lettuce with shredded carrot and red cabbage to gourmet blends with radicchio (red-leafed Italian chicory), escarole (a variety of endive) and romaine lettuce. Prewashed spinach and coleslaw mixtures are also available.
- Purchase deli, canned, cooked, or frozen meats and seafood. Meat counters sell many types of precut raw items such as stir-fry pieces and fajita strips.
- Purchase precut fresh fruit and vegetables. Canned and frozen fruits and vegetables can be used as well.
- Purchase bottled salad dressings, packaged croutons and shredded cheese.
- Pasta, rice and grains can be cooked several days ahead of time and stored in the refrigerator.

Wild Rice and Turkey Salad

Asian Beef Salad (page 30), Summer Garden Beef Salad

2

Meat Salads

Summer Garden Beef Salad

Make this salad when you have access to fresh basil, either from the garden or the farmer's market. Resist the urge to make it if fresh basil is not available; dried basil just doesn't deliver the needed flavor in this dish.

Green Onion Dressing (right)
3 cups julienne strips cooked lean roast beef (about 1¹/₂ pounds)
2 cups cooked fresh, frozen (thawed) or canned (drained) whole kernel corn (about 4 medium ears)
1 cup julienne strips cooked Chinese pea pods (about 4 ounces)
1 cup julienne strips roma (plum) tomatoes
1 cup julienne strips zucchini (about 1 medium)
1 cup julienne strips yellow bell pepper (about 1 small)
¹/₄ cup chopped fresh basil leaves
6 Bibb or Boston lettuce leaves
1 tablespoon chopped fresh chives

Prepare Green Onion Dressing. Toss dressing and remaining ingredients except lettuce leaves and chives. Serve salad on lettuce leaves. Sprinkle with chives.   **6 servings**

Green Onion Dressing

¹/₂ cup chopped green onions (about 5 medium)
¹/₂ cup plain nonfat yogurt
¹/₄ cup white wine or apple juice
¹/₄ cup beef broth
2 tablespoons lemon juice
¹/₄ teaspoon salt
¹/₄ teaspoon pepper

Place all ingredients in blender. Cover and blend about 30 seconds or until smooth.

SERVING SIZE: 1 Serving 360 Calories (160 Calories from Fat); Fat 18 g (Saturated 7 g); Cholesterol 90 mg; Sodium 220 mg; Carbohydrate 16 g; (Dietary Fiber 2 g); Protein 34 g; *% Daily Value:* Vitamin A 14%; Vitamin C 90%; Calcium 10%; Iron 26%

Asian Beef Salad

Although this salad requires a lot of chopping, it looks impressive when arranged on a platter and is also delicious. It's a great dish for company, or when you'd like to set a pretty table.

Tomato-Ginger Sauce (below)
1 package (about 7 ounces) rice stick
    noodles
Egg Strips (right)
2 cups 2-inch strips cooked lean beef
    steak (about 1 pound)
1 1/2 cups sliced seeded peeled cucumbers
    (about 1 1/2 medium)
2 tablespoons finely chopped unsalted
    roasted peanuts

Prepare Tomato-Ginger Sauce. Cook noodles as directed on package; drain. Prepare Egg Strips. Arrange noodles in center of plate or platter; top with sauce. Arrange beef, cucumbers and Egg Strips around noodles on plate. Sprinkle with peanuts.   **6 servings**

Tomato-Ginger Sauce

2 cups chopped tomatoes (about 2 large)
1/3 cup chopped green onions (about
    3 medium)
2 tablespoons chopped fresh cilantro
1 tablespoon balsamic vinegar
2 teaspoons finely chopped gingerroot
1 teaspoon sesame oil
1/4 teaspoon crushed red pepper
1 clove garlic, finely chopped

Mix all ingredients in glass or plastic bowl. Cover and refrigerate 1 hour.

Egg Strips

1/2 cup cholesterol-free egg product or egg
    substitute
1 tablespoon chopped fresh cilantro
1/8 teaspoon salt

Spray 8-inch skillet with nonstick cooking spray. Heat skillet over medium heat. Mix ingredients. Pour 1/4 cup egg mixture into skillet. Cook until egg mixture is set. Turn out onto cutting board; cut into 6 strips. Repeat with remaining egg mixture.

SERVING SIZE: 1 Serving 250 Calories (70 Calories from Fat); Fat 8 g (Saturated 3 g); Cholesterol 40 mg; Sodium 130 mg; Carbohydrate 25 g; (Dietary Fiber 2 g); Protein 20 g; *% Daily Value:* Vitamin A 8%; Vitamin C 40%; Calcium 4%; Iron 16%

Beef Teriyaki Salad

1/2 cup mayonnaise or salad dressing
2 tablespoons teriyaki sauce
2 cups cooked rice
3/4 pound cooked beef, cut into 2×1×1/8-inch
    pieces
4 ounces mushrooms, sliced, or 1 jar
    (2.5 ounces) sliced mushrooms, drained
4 ounces fresh Chinese pea pods or
    1 package (6 ounces) frozen Chinese
    pea pods, thawed and drained
3 green onions (with tops), sliced

Mix mayonnaise and teriyaki sauce in large bowl. Add remaining ingredients; toss until coated. Cover and refrigerate at least 1 hour.

                          4 servings

SERVING SIZE: 1 Serving 410 Calories (225 Calories from Fat); Fat 25 g (Saturated 5 g); Cholesterol 55 mg; Sodium 540 mg; Carbohydrate 28 g; (Dietary Fiber 1 g); Protein 19 g; *% Daily Value:* Vitamin A 2%; Vitamin C 26%; Calcium 4%; Iron 20%

Beef and Eggplant Salad

1 cup water
$1/2$ teaspoon salt
**1 medium eggplant (about $1\frac{1}{2}$ pounds),
    cut into $3/4$-inch cubes**
3 tablespoons olive or vegetable oil
2 tablespoons lemon juice
**1 tablespoon chopped fresh or 1 teaspoon
    dried oregano leaves**
$1/2$ teaspoon salt
$1/4$ teaspoon pepper
**1 pound cold roast beef, cut into julienne
    strips**
1 tablespoon chopped fresh parsley
1 medium tomato, cut into 8 wedges
8 Greek or large pitted ripe olives

Heat water and $1/2$ teaspoon salt to boiling in 3-quart saucepan. Add eggplant cubes. Cover and heat to boiling; reduce heat. Simmer about 10 minutes or until tender; drain.

Place eggplant in glass or plastic bowl. Mix oil, lemon juice, oregano, $1/2$ teaspoon salt and the pepper. Pour over eggplant; toss. Cover and refrigerate at least 5 hours.

Arrange beef strips on platter or 8 serving plates on lettuce leaves, if desired. Top with eggplant. Sprinkle eggplant with parsley. Garnish with tomato wedges and olives. **8 servings, about $3/4$ cup each**

SERVING SIZE: 1 Serving 210 Calories (125 Calories from Fat); Fat 14 g (Saturated 4 g); Cholesterol 45 mg; Sodium 350 mg; Carbohydrate 6 g; (Dietary Fiber 1 g); Protein 16 g; *% Daily Value:* Vitamin A 2%; Vitamin C 8%; Calcium 2%; Iron 12%

Beef-Potato Salad

$1\frac{1}{2}$ pounds small new potatoes
**$1/2$ pound sliced cooked roast beef, cut into
    thin strips**
1 small red onion, thinly sliced
1 small red bell pepper, thinly sliced
**1 small bunch green leaf lettuce, torn into
    bite-size pieces**
Red Wine Vinaigrette (below)

Place potatoes in 2-quart saucepan; add enough water to cover. Heat to boiling; reduce heat to medium. Cook uncovered 10 to 12 minutes or until potatoes are tender; drain. Cut potatoes into fourths. Mix potatoes and remaining ingredients except Red Wine Vinaigrette in large serving bowl. Toss with vinaigrette. Serve warm or cold.

4 servings

Red Wine Vinaigrette

$1/4$ cup olive or vegetable oil
2 tablespoons red wine vinegar
**1 tablespoon chopped fresh or 1 teaspoon
    dried thyme leaves**
$1/4$ teaspoon salt
$1/8$ teaspoon ground red pepper (cayenne)

Shake all ingredients in tightly covered container.

SERVING SIZE: 1 Serving 486 Calories (280 Calories from Fat); Fat 31 g (Saturated 3 g); Cholesterol 40 mg; Sodium 190 mg; Carbohydrate 38 g; (Dietary Fiber 4 g); Protein 17 g; *% Daily Value:* Vitamin A 20%; Vitamin C 30%; Calcium 4%; Iron 24%

Spicy Beef Salad

The Oriental influence in this salad is unmistakable as it uses rice wine vinegar, soy sauce, gingerroot and sesame oil.

1 pound beef flank steak or boneless
    sirloin steak
2 tablespoons sherry
1 tablespoon soy sauce
2 teaspoons sugar
$1/2$ cup thinly sliced green onions (with
    tops)
2 medium tomatoes, cut into chunks
4 cups sliced mushrooms (about 10
    ounces)
6 cups shredded lettuce (about 1 small
    head) or radicchio (about 2 small heads)
Spicy Dressing (right)

Trim fat from beef steak; cut beef with grain into 2-inch strips. Cut strips across grain into $1/8$-inch slices. (For ease in cutting, partially freeze beef, about $1 1/2$ hours.) Toss beef, sherry, soy sauce and sugar in glass or plastic bowl or in heavy plastic bag. Cover and refrigerate 30 minutes.

Heat 10-inch nonstick skillet over medium-high heat until 1 or 2 drops of water bubble and skitter when sprinkled on surface. Add half of the beef; stir-fry until beef is no longer pink, about 3 minutes. Remove beef from skillet; drain. Repeat with remaining beef; toss beef with green onions in large bowl.

Layer tomatoes, mushrooms and lettuce over beef. Cover and refrigerate at least 1 hour but no longer than 10 hours.

Pour Spicy Dressing over salad; toss until well coated. **6 servings, about $1 1/2$ cups each**

Spicy Dressing

$1/4$ cup rice wine or white wine vinegar
2 tablespoons soy sauce
1 teaspoon finely chopped gingerroot
1 teaspoon sesame oil
$1/8$ teaspoon ground red pepper
1 clove garlic, finely chopped

Shake all ingredients in tightly covered container.

SERVING SIZE: 1 Serving 160 Calories (55 Calories from Fat); Fat 6 g (Saturated 2 g); Cholesterol 40 mg; Sodium 560 mg; Carbohydrate 9 g; (Dietary Fiber 1 g); Protein 18 g; *% Daily Value:* Vitamin A 4%; Vitamin C 22%; Calcium 2%; Iron 14%

Zesty Dressings

Try these easy dressings to make any salad special.

- Cheese-Olive Dressing: Mix 1 package (3 ounces) cream cheese, softened, and $1/4$ cup half-and-half; stir in $1/4$ cup chopped ripe or pimiento-stuffed olives.
- Chili Dressing: Mix 1 carton (6 ounces) 100% natural plain yogurt, 1 table-spoon chili sauce and 1 teaspoon onion salt.
- Cucumber Dressing: Mix $1/4$ medium cucumber, chopped (about $1/2$ cup), $1/4$ cup dairy sour cream, $1/4$ cup mayonnaise or salad dressing and $1/2$ teaspoon salt.
- Curry Dressing: Mix $1/2$ cup Italian dressing, $1/4$ teaspoon curry powder and dash of ground red pepper.
- Dill Dressing: Mix $1/2$ cup French dressing and $1/2$ teaspoon dried dill weed.
- Red and White Dressing: Use $1/2$ to $3/4$ cup blue cheese dressing to top salad. Drizzle with French dressing.

Fajita Salad

Here's a low-calorie version of a favorite Tex-Mex dish.

Corn Chips (right)
³/₄-pound lean beef boneless sirloin steak
2 teaspoons vegetable oil
2 medium bell peppers, cut into strips
1 small onion, thinly sliced
1 tablespoon vegetable oil
3 tablespoons red wine vinegar
1 tablespoon lime juice
1 teaspoon chopped fresh or ¹/₂ teaspoon dried oregano leaves
³/₄ teaspoon chili powder
¹/₄ teaspoon salt
1 clove garlic, finely chopped
4 cups bite-size pieces greens (spinach, romaine, iceberg lettuce)
¹/₄ cup plain nonfat yogurt

Prepare Corn Chips. Trim fat from beef steak. Cut beef with grain into 2-inch strips. Cut strips across grain into ¹/₈-inch slices. Heat 2 teaspoons oil in 10-inch nonstick skillet over medium-high heat. Sauté beef about 3 minutes, or until no longer pink. Remove beef from skillet. Add bell peppers and onion to skillet. Sauté about 3 minutes, or until crisp-tender. Mix beef and vegetables.

Shake remaining ingredients except greens and yogurt in tightly covered container. Place greens on serving plate. Top with beef mixture. Pour dressing over salad. Top with yogurt. Serve with Corn Chips.   **4 servings**

Corn Chips

4 corn tortillas (about 6 inches in diameter)
1 tablespoon reduced-calorie margarine, melted
¹/₈ teaspoon salt

Heat oven to 400°. Brush tortillas with margarine; sprinkle with salt. Cut each tortilla into 10 pieces. Arrange in ungreased jelly roll pan, 15¹/₂ × 10¹/₂ × 1 inch. Bake 5 to 6 minutes or until crisp. (Chips will crisp as they cool.)

SERVING SIZE: 1 Serving 170 Calories (70 Calories from Fat); Fat 8 g (Saturated 2 g); Cholesterol 40 mg; Sodium 190 mg; Carbohydrate 8 g; (Dietary Fiber 1 g); Protein 17 g; *% Daily Value:* Vitamin A 6%; Vitamin C 30%; Calcium 6%; Iron 12%

Snappy Salad Greens

The difference between a crisp, lively tossed salad and one that's limp and soggy may be simply a matter of how you treat the greens. Wash before you store, discarding wilted or discolored leaves. Drain, dry and refrigerate in the crisper, a plastic bag or a covered container. Then for quick work at mealtime, just tear the greens into bite-size pieces with your fingers and toss at the last minute with only enough dressing to coat the leaves.

Broiled Sirloin and Mushroom Salad

1¹/₂-pound beef boneless sirloin steak,
   1¹/₂ inches thick
1 jar (4.5 ounces) sliced mushrooms,
   drained
1 medium red or green pepper, cut into
   thin strips
¹/₃ cup red wine vinegar
¹/₄ cup vegetable oil
1 teaspoon salt
1 teaspoon snipped fresh tarragon leaves
   or ¹/₄ teaspoon dried tarragon leaves
¹/₂ teaspoon Worcestershire sauce
¹/₄ teaspoon pepper
2 cloves garlic, crushed
Salad greens
Cherry or yellow pear tomatoes

Slash outer edge of fat on beef steak diagonally at 1-inch intervals to prevent curling (do not cut into lean). Set oven control to broil. Place beef on rack in broiler pan. Broil with top about 2 inches from heat until medium, about 13 minutes on each side. Cool beef; cut into ³/₈-inch strips.

Arrange in ungreased rectangular baking dish, 13 × 9 × 2 inches. Place mushrooms on beef; top with pepper strips.

Mix remaining ingredients except salad greens and tomatoes; pour over beef and vegetables. Cover and refrigerate at least 3 hours, spooning marinade over vegetables occasionally.

Remove beef and vegetables with slotted spoon onto salad greens; garnish with tomatoes.

4 servings

SERVING SIZE: 1 Serving 315 Calories (170 Calories from Fat); Fat 19 g (Saturated 4 g); Cholesterol 80 mg; Sodium 710 mg; Carbohydrate 6 g; (Dietary Fiber 1 g); Protein 31 g; *% Daily Value:* Vitamin A 16%; Vitamin C 76%; Calcium 2%; Iron 19%

Tangy Steak Salad

This warm, hearty salad is perfect on a cold evening.

1 tablespoon olive or vegetable oil
1 pound beef boneless top sirloin steak,
   thinly sliced
3 tablespoons Dijon mustard
1 tablespoon chopped fresh parsley
4 cups bite-size pieces iceberg lettuce
1 cup sliced celery
4 green onions (with tops), sliced
1 small red bell pepper, sliced
Tangy Dressing (below)

Heat oil in 10-inch skillet over high heat until hot. Cook beef steak about 2 minutes, stirring constantly, until brown; drain. Stir in mustard and parsley; keep warm. Toss lettuce, celery, green onions and bell pepper. Divide among 4 dinner plates. Top with steak mixture. Serve with Tangy Dressing.

4 servings

Tangy Dressing

³/₄ cup water
2 teaspoons cornstarch
3 tablespoons vinegar
2 tablespoons olive or vegetable oil
1 tablespoon ketchup
1 tablespoon Dijon mustard
1 teaspoon chopped fresh or ¹/₂ teaspoon
   dried basil
³/₄ teaspoon salt

Mix water and cornstarch in 1-quart saucepan. Heat to boiling over medium heat, stirring frequently, until mixture thickens. Cook and stir 1 minute. Stir in remaining ingredients. Heat until warm.

SERVING SIZE: 1 Serving 240 Calories (125 Calories from Fat); Fat 14 g (Saturated 3 g); Cholesterol 55 mg; Sodium 700 mg; Carbohydrate 8 g; (Dietary Fiber 1 g); Protein 22 g; *% Daily Value:* Vitamin A 10%; Vitamin C 50%; Calcium 4%; Iron 16%

Tangy Steak Salad

Taco Salads

For a low-fat variation, substitute ground turkey for the ground beef and nonfat yogurt for the Thousand Island Dressing, and omit the avocado. You reduce the fat by more than 50 percent and the calories by about 35 percent!

Tortilla Shells (right)
1 pound ground beef
²/₃ cup water
1 tablespoon chili powder
¹/₂ teaspoon salt
¹/₄ teaspoon garlic powder
¹/₄ teaspoon ground red pepper (cayenne)
1 can (15¹/₂ ounces) kidney beans, drained (reserve empty can)
1 medium head lettuce, torn into bite-size pieces (about 10 cups)
1 cup shredded Cheddar cheese (4 ounces)
²/₃ cup sliced ripe olives
2 medium tomatoes, coarsely chopped
1 medium onion, chopped (about ¹/₂ cup)
³/₄ cup Thousand Island Dressing or bottled dressing
1 avocado, thinly sliced
Sour cream

Prepare Tortilla Shells. Cook ground beef in 10-inch skillet, stirring occasionally, until brown; drain. Stir in water, chili powder, salt, garlic powder, red pepper and kidney beans. Heat to boiling; reduce heat. Simmer uncovered 15 minutes, stirring occasionally; cool 10 minutes.

Mix lettuce, cheese, olives, tomatoes and onion in large bowl. Toss with Thousand Island Dressing. Pour ground beef mixture over top; toss. Divide among Tortilla Shells. Garnish with avocado and sour cream. Serve immediately.

8 servings

Tortilla Shells

Vegetable oil
8 flour tortillas (10-inch diameter)

Remove label and both ends of reserved kidney bean can. Wash and dry can. Heat oil (1¹/₂ inches) in 3-quart saucepan to 375°. (Diameter of saucepan should be at least 9 inches.) Place 1 tortilla on top of saucepan. Place can on center of tortilla with long-handled tongs. Push tortilla into oil by gently pushing can down. Fry tortilla about 5 seconds or until set; remove can with tongs. Fry tortilla 1 to 2 minutes longer, turning tortilla in oil, until tortilla is crisp and golden brown. Carefully remove tortilla from oil and drain excess oil from inside. Turn tortilla shell upside down; cool. Repeat with remaining tortillas.

TO MICROWAVE: Crumble ground beef into 2-quart microwavable casserole. Cover loosely and microwave on high 6 to 7 minutes, stirring after 3 minutes, until no pink remains; drain. Reduce water to ¹/₄ cup. Stir in water, chili powder, salt, garlic powder, red pepper and kidney beans. Cover loosely and microwave on high 2 to 3 minutes or until boiling. Continue as directed.

SERVING SIZE: 1 Serving 595 Calories (360 Calories from Fat); Fat 40 g (Saturated 14 g); Cholesterol 70 mg; Sodium 900 mg; Carbohydrate 42 g; (Dietary Fiber 6 g); Protein 23 g; *% Daily Value:* Vitamin A 16%; Vitamin C 20%; Calcium 18%; Iron 26%

Southwestern Pork Salad

³/₄ pound pork tenderloin
¹/₄ teaspoon salt
¹/₄ teaspoon pepper
8 cups bite-size pieces mixed salad
  greens or 1 package (4 ounces) mixed
  greens
1 medium yellow bell pepper, sliced
¹/₂ pound mushrooms, sliced
1 can (15 to 16 ounces) black-eyed peas,
  rinsed and drained
Creamy Lime Dressing (below)

Heat oven to 350°. Place tenderloin on rack in shallow roasting pan. Sprinkle with salt and pepper. Insert meat thermometer horizontally so that tip is in thickest part of pork. Bake uncovered 30 to 40 minutes or until thermometer registers 160° (medium doneness). Cool pork; cut into slices. Arrange greens, bell pepper, mushrooms, peas and pork on large serving plate. Serve with Creamy Lime Dressing.   **4 servings**

Creamy Lime Dressing

  ¹/₂ cup nonfat sour cream
  ¹/₄ cup chopped fresh cilantro
  2 tablespoons lime juice
  2 tablespoons vegetable oil
  ¹/₄ teaspoon salt

Mix all ingredients.

SERVING SIZE: 1 Serving 330 Calories (110 Calories from Fat); Fat 12 g (Saturated 4 g); Cholesterol 90 mg; Sodium 585 mg; Carbohydrate 30 g; (Dietary Fiber 11 g); Protein 36 g; % *Daily Value:* Vitamin A 38%; Vitamin C 40%; Calcium 12%; Iron 36%

Warm Pork and Bulgur Salad with Apricots

Apricots add a bright burst of flavor to this satisfying salad.

  1 small onion, chopped
  2 tablespoons margarine or butter
  1 can (10 ³/₄ ounces) condensed chicken
   broth
  ¹/₂ broth can water
  1 cup uncooked bulgur
  ¹/₂ teaspoon salt
  2 cups bite-size pieces cooked pork
  ¹/₂ cup snipped dried apricots
  ¹/₄ cup oil-and-vinegar dressing
  2 stalks celery, sliced
  Salad greens

Cook and stir onion in margarine in 3-quart saucepan until tender. Add broth, water, bulgur and salt. Heat to boiling; reduce heat.

Cover and simmer 15 minutes. Remove from heat; stir in pork, apricots, dressing and celery. Spoon onto salad greens.   **4 servings**

CHILLED PORK AND BULGUR SALAD: Cover and refrigerate at least 2 hours. Just before serving, stir in 2 tablespoons additional oil-and-vinegar dressing.

SERVING SIZE: 1 Serving 500 Calories (200 Calories from Fat); Fat 22 g (Saturated 5 g); Cholesterol 60 mg; Sodium 1,000 mg; Carbohydrate 57 g; (Dietary Fiber 12 g); Protein 31 g; % *Daily Value:* Vitamin A 22%; Vitamin C 10%; Calcium 6%; Iron 18%

Pork and Mango Salad

If you like, use skinless chicken instead of pork, and you'll save about 45 calories per serving.

1 large mango or papaya
1/2 cup plain nonfat yogurt
1 teaspoon sugar
1/4 teaspoon ground ginger
4 cups shredded Boston or iceberg lettuce
2 cups julienne strips cooked lean pork (about 8 ounces)
1 cup orange sections (about 2 medium)
1/2 avocado, peeled and thinly sliced

Cut mango in half and peel. Mash enough mango to measure 1/4 cup; cut remaining mango into thin slices. Mix mashed mango, yogurt, sugar and ginger.

Place 1 cup lettuce on each of 4 salad plates. Arrange mango slices, pork, oranges and avocado on lettuce. Top each salad with mango mixture. **4 servings**

SERVING SIZE: 1 Serving 270 Calories (100 Calories from Fat); Fat 11 g (Saturated 3 g); Cholesterol 60 mg; Sodium 65 mg; Carbohydrate 23 g; (Dietary Fiber 4 g); Protein 24 g; *% Daily Value:* Vitamin A 24%; Vitamin C 88%; Calcium 10%; Iron 8%

Bacon and Tomato Salad

Cucumber Yogurt Dressing (right)
Salad greens
6 plum tomatoes, sliced, or 3 medium tomatoes, cut into wedges
1 pound bacon, crisply cooked and crumbled
1 cup plain or seasoned croutons

Prepare Cucumber Yogurt Dressing. Arrange salad greens, tomatoes and bacon on 4 salad plates; sprinkle with croutons. Serve with dressing. **4 servings**

Cucumber Yogurt Dressing

1 cup plain yogurt
1/2 cup chopped cucumber
1 1/2 teaspoons sugar
1 teaspoon prepared horseradish
1/2 teaspoon salt
1 green onion, thinly sliced

Mix all ingredients. Cover and refrigerate until ready to serve.

SERVING SIZE: 1 Serving 295 Calories (160 Calories from Fat); Fat 18 g (Saturated 7 g); Cholesterol 30 mg; Sodium 890 mg; Carbohydrate 20 g; (Dietary Fiber 2 g); Protein 15 g; *% Daily Value:* Vitamin A 12%; Vitamin C 70%; Calcium 14%; Iron 10%

Winter Fruit Salad with Ham and Walnuts

1/4 cup sour cream
1/4 cup mayonnaise or salad dressing
1/2 teaspoon ground ginger
2 cups cut-up fully cooked smoked ham
1/2 cup snipped dates (about 3 ounces)
1/2 cup walnut pieces
2 medium unpeeled eating apples, cut into wedges
2 medium oranges, peeled, cut into halves and sliced
1 package (6 ounces) shredded Swiss cheese (about 1 1/2 cups)
Salad greens

Mix sour cream, mayonnaise and ginger in large bowl. Toss with remaining ingredients except salad greens. Serve on salad greens. **6 servings**

SERVING SIZE: 1 Serving 430 Calories (250 Calories from Fat); Fat 28 g (Saturated 10 g); Cholesterol 65 mg; Sodium 840 mg; Carbohydrate 27 g; (Dietary Fiber 3 g); Protein 21 g; *% Daily Value:* Vitamin A 10%; Vitamin C 32%; Calcium 32%; Iron 8%

Pork and Mango Salad

Muffuletta Salad

Muffuletta Salad

Named after the famous Muffuletta sand-wich from New Orleans, this salad show-cases the sandwich's savory filling.

  Olive-Tomato Dressing (below)
  2 cups uncooked mostaccioli
  1 tablespoon olive oil
  1/4 pound sliced salami, cut into 1/8-inch
    strips
  1/4 pound thinly sliced fully cooked
    smoked ham, cut into 1/8-inch strips
  1/4 pound provolone cheese, cut into
    1/8-inch strips
  Salad greens

Prepare Olive-Tomato Dressing. Cook mostaccioli as directed on package; drain. Rinse in cold water; drain. Toss mostaccioli and oil.

Layer mostaccioli, salami, ham, provolone and salad greens on Olive-Tomato Dressing. Cover and refrigerate at least 4 hours but no longer than 24 hours. Toss just before serving. Arrange on salad greens.   **6 servings**

Olive-Tomato Dressing

  1 anchovy fillet, mashed
  1 large clove garlic, crushed
  1/3 cup olive oil
  1 cup cherry tomatoes, cut into halves
  1/2 cup chopped pimiento-stuffed olives
  1/2 cup chopped Greek or ripe olives
  1/2 cup chopped mixed pickled vegetables
  1/2 teaspoon dried oregano leaves

Stir anchovy and garlic thoroughly into oil in large bowl. Stir in remaining ingredients.

SERVING SIZE: 1 Serving 470 Calories (250 Calories from Fat); Fat 28 g (Saturated 8 g); Cholesterol 40 mg; Sodium 1,190 mg; Carbohydrate 38 g; (Dietary Fiber 2 g); Protein 18 g; *% Daily Value:* Vitamin A 10%; Vitamin C 26%; Calcium 18%; Iron 20%

Chef's Salad

Use your favorite ingredients in this salad—you are the chef!

  1/2 cup julienne strips cooked meat (beef,
    smoked ham or tongue)
  1/2 cup julienne strips cooked chicken or
    turkey
  1/2 cup julienne strips Swiss cheese
  4 green onions (with tops), chopped
    (about 1/2 cup)
  1 medium head lettuce, torn into bite-size
    pieces
  1 small bunch romaine, torn into bite-size
    pieces
  1 medium stalk celery, sliced (about
    1/2 cup)
  1/2 cup mayonnaise or salad dressing
  1/4 cup French dressing
  2 hard-cooked eggs, sliced
  2 tomatoes, cut into wedges

Reserve a few strips of meat, chicken and cheese. Mix remaining meat, chicken and cheese, the onions, lettuce, romaine and celery. Mix mayonnaise and French dressing. Pour over lettuce mixture and toss. Top with reserved meat, chicken and cheese strips, the eggs and tomatoes.   **5 servings**

SERVING SIZE: 1 Serving 380 Calories (280 Calories from Fat); Fat 31 g (Saturated 8 g); Cholesterol 140 mg; Sodium 610 mg; Carbohydrate 11 g; (Dietary Fiber 2 g); Protein 16 g; *% Daily Value:* Vitamin A 30%; Vitamin C 56%; Calcium 20%; Iron 14%

Prosciutto Salad with Grapefruit-Honey Dressing

Prosciutto Salad with Grapefruit-Honey Dressing

2 grapefruit
Grapefruit-Honey dressing (below)
¹/₂ pound prosciutto or thinly sliced fully cooked smoked ham
Salad greens
3 unpeeled eating apples, sliced

Peel and section grapefruit, allowing juice to drain into bowl. Reserve ¹/₄ cup of the juice for Grapefruit-Honey Dressing; prepare dressing. Roll up prosciutto.

Arrange salad greens on platter or 4 salad plates. Arrange grapefruit, apples and prosciutto on greens. Serve with dressing.   **4 servings**

Grapefruit-Honey Dressing

¹/₄ cup reserved grapefruit juice
3 tablespoons honey
3 tablespoons vegetable oil or sour cream
¹/₄ teaspoon celery seed

Shake all ingredients in tightly covered container. Shake before using.

SERVING SIZE: 1 Serving 360 Calories (Calories from 160 Fat); Fat 18 g (Saturated 4 g); Cholesterol 30 mg; Sodium 440 mg; Carbohydrate 43 g; (Dietary Fiber 4 g); Protein 11 g; *% Daily Value:* Vitamin A 6%; Vitamin C 100%; Calcium 4%; Iron 6%

Ham Salad with Cheddar Dressing

3 cups bite-size pieces salad greens
1¹/₂ cups frozen green peas, thawed and drained
³/₄ pound fully cooked smoked ham, cut into ¹/₂-inch cubes (about 2 cups)
¹/₂ head cauliflower, broken into flowerets
¹/₂ small red onion, thinly sliced
Cheddar Dressing (below)

Toss all ingredients except Cheddar Dressing. Serve with dressing and freshly ground pepper, if desired.   **6 servings**

Cheddar Dressing

1 cup shredded Cheddar cheese (4 ounces)
¹/₄ cup milk
2 tablespoons wine vinegar
¹/₄ teaspoon salt
1 package (3 ounces) cream cheese, softened
1 clove garlic

Place all ingredients in workbowl of food processor fitted with steel blade or in blender container. Cover and process, stopping once to scrape down sides, until mixture is of uniform consistency, about 30 seconds.

SERVING SIZE: 1 Serving 270 Calories (155 Calories from Fat); Fat 17 g (Saturated 9 g); Cholesterol 70 mg; Sodium 1,150 mg; Carbohydrate 10 g; (Dietary Fiber 3 g); Protein 22 g; *% Daily Value:* Vitamin A 12%; Vitamin C 66%; Calcium 14%; Iron 10%

Mexicali Pasta Salad

3

Meatless Salads

Mexicali Pasta Salad

8 ounces uncooked tricolor pasta spirals
   (about 3 cups)
6 small tomatillos, each cut into 8 wedges
$\frac{1}{2}$ jalapeño chili, seeded and finely
   chopped
1 can (20 ounces) pineapple chunks in
   juice, drained (reserve 2 tablespoons
   juice)
1 tablespoon snipped fresh cilantro
2 tablespoons vegetable oil
$\frac{1}{2}$ teaspoon grated lime peel
$\frac{1}{4}$ teaspoon salt

Cook pasta as directed on package; drain. Rinse with cold water; drain. Mix pasta, tomatillos, chili and pineapple.

Mix reserved pineapple juice and the remaining ingredients. Pour over pasta mixture; toss. Cover and refrigerate until chilled, at least 2 hours. **6 servings**

SERVING SIZE: 1 Serving 260 Calories (55 Calories from Fat); Fat 6 g (Saturated 1 g); Cholesterol 0 mg; Sodium 100 mg; Carbohydrate 48 g; (Dietary Fiber 3 g); Protein 6 g; *% Daily Value:* Vitamin A 10%; Vitamin C 56%; Calcium 2%; Iron 12%

Pimiento Pasta Salad

2 cups cooked rotini or spiral macaroni
2 cups thinly sliced zucchini (about
   1 medium)
1 tablespoon snipped fresh basil leaves or
   1 teaspoon dried basil leaves
1 tablespoon white wine vinegar
1 teaspoon lemon juice
$\frac{1}{4}$ teaspoon coarsely cracked pepper
1 clove garlic, finely chopped
1 jar (4 ounces) pimiento strips, undrained
1 tablespoon grated Parmesan cheese

Mix all ingredients except cheese. Cover and refrigerate at least 2 hours. Sprinkle with Parmesan cheese. **6 servings, about $\frac{2}{3}$ cup each**

SERVING SIZE: 1 Serving 80 Calories (10 Calories from Fat); Fat 1 g (Saturated 0 g); Cholesterol 0 mg; Sodium 20 mg; Carbohydrate 16 g; (Dietary Fiber 1 g); Protein 3 g; *% Daily Value:* Vitamin A 6%; Vitamin C 30%; Calcium 2%; Iron 6%

Northern Italian White Bean Salad

Slices of Italian bread brushed lightly with olive oil and broiled are delicious with this tasty bean salad.

1 cup coarsely chopped seeded tomato
   (about 1 large)
1/2 cup chopped red onion (about
   1/2 medium)
1/2 cup chopped bell pepper (about 1 small)
1/4 cup chopped fresh parsley
1/4 cup vegetable or olive oil
2 tablespoons chopped fresh or
   2 teaspoons dried basil leaves
2 tablespoons red wine vinegar
1/2 teaspoon salt
1/8 teaspoon pepper
2 cans (19 ounces each) cannellini beans,
   rinsed and drained
12 leaves red leaf lettuce

Carefully mix all ingredients in glass or plastic bowl except lettuce. Cover and refrigerate at least 2 hours. Serve bean mixture on lettuce.

6 servings

SERVING SIZE: 1 Serving 350 Calories (90 Calories from Fat); Fat 10 g (Saturated 1 g); Cholesterol 0 mg; Sodium 620 mg; Carbohydrate 50 g; (Dietary Fiber 11 g); Protein 18 g; % *Daily Value:* Vitamin A 8%; Vitamin C 36%; Calcium 20%; Iron 42%

Greek Pasta Salad

4 cups cooked rosamarina (orzo) pasta
2 cups thinly sliced cucumber
3/4 cup chopped tomato (about 1 medium)
1/2 cup chopped green bell pepper (about
   1 small)
1/2 cup chopped red onion (about
   1/2 medium)
1/4 cup finely chopped fresh parsley
1/4 cup olive or vegetable oil
1/4 cup lemon juice
1/4 teaspoon salt
1 can (15 to 16 ounces) garbanzo beans,
   rinsed and drained
1 can (4 ounces) sliced ripe olives,
   drained*
1/2 cup crumbled feta cheese

Mix all ingredients except cheese in glass or plastic bowl. Cover and refrigerate at least 1 hour to blend flavors. Top with cheese.

5 servings

* 1/3 cup pitted, sliced kalamata or Greek olives can be substituted for the ripe olives.

SERVING SIZE: 1 Serving 440 Calories (160 Calories from Fat); Fat 18 g (Saturated 4 g); Cholesterol 10 mg; Sodium 780 mg; Carbohydrate 62 g; (Dietary Fiber 7 g); Protein 15 g; % *Daily Value:* Vitamin A 6%; Vitamin C 40%; Calcium 14%; Iron 28%

Greek Pasta Salad, Whole Wheat Fettuccine with Spring Vegetables (page 48)

Pasta for Salads

- All cooked pasta can be used interchangeably in salads, measure for measure. When using uncooked pasta, substitute a pasta close in shape and size or the cooked volume may vary due to weight differences.
- If pasta is to be used in cold salad, rinse it in cold water to prevent sticking together; drain well.
- For pasta to absorb maximum flavor, add salad dressing while pasta is still warm, then refrigerate.
- Small pastas perfect for salads: couscous, orzo (rosamarina), small shells and acini de pepe (dots).
- Medium pastas perfect for salads: fusilli (corkscrew-shaped), rotelle (wagon wheels), rotini (spirals), gemelli (two pieces twisted together), radatore (radiator-shaped), farfalle (bow ties), conchiglie (shells) and tortellini (stuffed).
- Long pastas perfect for salads: fettuccine, linguine, vermicelli and fusilli. Salads are easier to toss if you break long pastas in half or thirds before cooking.
- One ounce of uncooked pasta will yield approximately 1/2 cup of cooked pasta.

Whole Wheat Fettuccine with Spring Vegetables

1 package (12 ounces) whole wheat fettuccine
2 cups cut-up asparagus or 1 package (10 ounces) frozen asparagus cuts, thawed
2 cups julienne strips zucchini (about 2 medium)
1 package (10 ounces) frozen green peas, thawed
1 tablespoon margarine or butter
3/4 chopped tomato (about 1 medium)
1/4 cup chopped fresh or 2 tablespoons dried basil leaves
1/4 teaspoon pepper
1/2 cup grated Parmesan cheese

Cook fettuccine as directed on package; drain. Rinse in cold water; drain. Cook asparagus in margarine in 10-inch skillet about 4 minutes, stirring frequently, until crisp-tender. Add zucchini, cook and stir 2 minutes. Mix asparagus mixture, fettuccine, tomato, basil and pepper. Cover and refrigerate about 1 hour or until chilled. Serve with cheese. **6 servings**

SERVING SIZE: 1 Serving 290 Calories (65 Calories from Fat); Fat 7 g (Saturated 2 g); Cholesterol 55 mg; Sodium 430 mg; Carbohydrate 48 g; (Dietary Fiber 6 g); Protein 14 g; % *Daily Value:* Vitamin A 14%; Vitamin C 20%; Calcium 16%; Iron 24%

Gazpacho Pasta Salad

1 pound rotini pasta, cooked and drained
$1/2$ cup finely chopped fresh cilantro leaves
8 green onions, chopped (about $1/2$ cup)
2 large tomatoes, seeded and chopped
  (about 2 cups)
1 small red bell pepper, chopped (about
  $1/2$ cup)
1 small yellow bell pepper, chopped (about
  $1/2$ cup)
1 large cucumber, peeled and chopped
  (about $1^1/2$ cups)
1 green Anaheim chili, seeded and
  chopped (about $1/4$ cup)
Lime Vinaigrette (below)

Combine all ingredients in large bowl until well blended. Prepare and pour Lime Vinaigrette over salad; toss to coat.

Lime Vinaigrette

$1/2$ cup olive oil
$1/2$ cup lime juice
$1/2$ teaspoon salt
$1/4$ teaspoon pepper
2 cloves garlic, crushed
1 bottle (10 ounces) tomato juice

Mix all ingredients.

SERVING SIZE: 1 Serving 490 Calories (180 Calories from Fat); Fat 20 g (Saturated 3 g); Cholesterol 0 mg; Sodium 370 mg; Carbohydrate 70 g; (Dietary Fiber 4 g); Protein 12 g; *% Daily Value:* Vitamin A 24%; Vitamin C 100%; Calcium 4%; Iron 22%

Wheat Berry Salad with Vinaigrette Dressing

This salad is very versatile. Change the look and flavor by substituting other cooked whole grains for the wheat berries, or other beans for the garbanzos.

1 cup uncooked wheat berries
$2^1/2$ cups water
$1^1/2$ cups broccoli flowerets
$1/2$ cup chopped green onions (about
  5 medium)
$1/2$ cup chopped carrot (about 1 medium)
1 can (15 ounces) garbanzo beans,
  drained
Vinaigrette Dressing (below)

Heat wheat berries and water to boiling in 2-quart saucepan, stirring once or twice; reduce heat. Cover and simmer 50 to 60 minutes or until wheat berries are tender but still chewy; drain. Toss wheat berries and remaining ingredients in glass or plastic bowl. Cover and refrigerate at least 1 hour. **4 servings**

Vinaigrette Dressing

$1/4$ cup balsamic or cider vinegar
2 tablespoons olive or vegetable oil
1 tablespoon chopped fresh or 1 teaspoon
  dried basil leaves
$1/4$ teaspoon paprika
$1/8$ teaspoon salt
1 clove garlic, crushed

Mix all ingredients.

SERVING SIZE: 1 Serving 350 Calories (90 Calories from Fat); Fat 10 g (Saturated 2 g); Cholesterol 0 mg; Sodium 240 mg; Carbohydrate 52 g; (Dietary Fiber 10 g); Protein 13 g; *% Daily Value:* Vitamin A 26%; Vitamin C 24%; Calcium 8%; Iron 26%

Wheat Berry Salad (page 49), Black Bean Salad

Black Bean Salad

Chili Dressing (below)
1 cup frozen whole kernel corn, thawed
1 cup diced jicama
¾ cup chopped seeded tomato (about
    1 medium)
2 green onions (with tops), sliced
2 cans (15 ounces each) black beans,
    rinsed and drained

Toss all ingredients in large glass or plastic bowl. Cover and refrigerate at least 2 hours, stirring occasionally. **4 servings, about 1 cup each**

Chili Dressing

    ¼ cup red wine vinegar
    2 tablespoons vegetable oil
    ½ teaspoon chili powder
    ¼ teaspoon ground cumin
    1 small clove garlic, crushed

Mix all ingredients.

SERVING SIZE: 1 Serving 335 Calories (70 Calories from Fat); Fat 8 g (Saturated 1 g); Cholesterol 0 mg; Sodium 450 mg; Carbohydrate 63 g; (Dietary Fiber 15 g); Protein 18 g; *% Daily Value:* Vitamin A 4%; Vitamin C 28%; Calcium 14%; Iron 30%

Grow Your Own Sprouts

It's easy to sprout mung beans in your kitchen. Fold a piece of terry toweling or cheesecloth (about 16 × 8 inches) in fourths (8 × 4 inches). Place in loaf pan, 9½ × 5 × 3 inches. Pour water over the towel until it is saturated, then sprinkle ¼ cup dried green mung beans on top in a single layer. Cover with aluminum foil; let stand 24 hours.

Uncover the planter and set it in a dark, draft-free place. Water it each day as the top layer dries out. Beans will sprout in 2 or 3 days and will be ready to harvest in 4 to 6 days.

To harvest, snip the plants off at the base with scissors. Rinse to remove the husks and dry well. Place in a plastic bag; close tightly and refrigerate no longer than 3 days. The yield from ¼ cup dried mung beans is 3 cups sprouts.

Fireworks Salad

1 package (10 ounces) Chinese noodles,
  cooked and drained
1 medium yellow bell pepper, thinly sliced
1 medium red bell pepper, thinly sliced
1/2 pound sugar snap peas, cooked
1 cup shredded green cabbage
6 green onions, chopped (about 1/3 cup)
1 can (8 ounces) water chestnuts, drained
  and cut into fourths
3 tablespoons soy sauce
3 tablespoons dry sherry or chicken broth
2 tablespoons sesame oil
1 teaspoon sugar
1/2 to 1 teaspoon red pepper sauce

Mix noodles, bell peppers, peas, cabbage,
onions and water chestnuts in large bowl. Whisk
together remaining ingredients; pour over vegetable mixture and toss to coat. Cover and
refrigerate at least 1 hour to blend flavors.

8 servings

SERVING SIZE: 1 Serving 150 Calories (35 Calories from
Fat); Fat 4 g (Saturated 1 g); Cholesterol 0 mg; Sodium
400 mg; Carbohydrate 28 g; (Dietary Fiber 2 g); Protein 3 g;
% Daily Value: Vitamin A 10%; Vitamin C 90%; Calcium 4%;
Iron 8%

Spicy Brown Rice and Pinto Bean Salad

*The crisp crunch of vegetables stands up
well to the fresh flavor of this dressing.
Serve the salad with a slotted spoon and
place it on a bed of shredded lettuce
or in lettuce cups for a more elegant
presentation.*

4 cups cooked brown rice
2 cups cooked pinto beans or 1 can
  (15 ounces) pinto beans, drained
1 cup chopped tomato (about 1 large)
1 cup chopped cucumber (about
  1 medium)
1 cup chopped jicama (about 1/2 medium)
1/2 cup chopped green bell pepper (about
  1 small)
1/4 cup chopped pepperocini (Italian
  bottled peppers) or green chilies
3 tablespoons chopped fresh cilantro
  leaves
2 tablespoons lemon juice
1 tablespoon Dijon mustard
1 teaspoon vegetable oil
1/2 teaspoon salt
2 ounces hot pepper Monterey Jack or
  Cheddar cheese, cut into 1/4-inch cubes

Mix all ingredients in glass or plastic bowl. Cover
and refrigerate at least 2 hours or until chilled.

6 servings

SERVING SIZE: 1 Serving 315 Calories (55 Calories from
Fat); Fat 6 g (Saturated 3 g); Cholesterol 10 mg; Sodium
280 mg; Carbohydrate 53 g; (Dietary Fiber 8 g); Protein
12 g; % Daily Value: Vitamin A 6%; Vitamin C 28%;
Calcium 10%; Iron 16%

Kasha Tabbouleh

Serve this salad on a bed of fresh spinach, and add milk, cottage cheese or yogurt if you'd like to increase the protein content.

2 cups water
1 package (6¹/₂ ounces) roasted
    buckwheat kernels (kasha)
1¹/₂ cups finely chopped fresh parsley
1¹/₂ cups chopped seeded tomatoes (about
    2 medium)
¹/₃ cup chopped onion (about 1 medium)
¹/₄ cup chopped fresh or 2 teaspoons dried
    mint leaves
1 small cucumber, peeled and chopped
1 can (15 to 16 ounces) garbanzo beans,
    rinsed and drained
¹/₄ cup lemon juice
1 tablespoon honey
2 teaspoons Dijon mustard
¹/₄ teaspoon pepper
Lettuce leaves

Heat water to boiling in 2-quart saucepan. Stir in buckwheat kernels. Heat to boiling; reduce heat. Cover and simmer about 25 minutes or until water is absorbed and buckwheat is tender.

Mix buckwheat, parsley, tomatoes, onion, mint, cucumber and beans in glass or plastic bowl. Mix remaining ingredients except salad greens; toss with buckwheat mixture. Cover and refrigerate at least 1 hour. Serve on salad greens.

4 servings

SERVING SIZE: 1 Serving 245 Calories (25 Calories from Fat); Fat 3 g (Saturated 1 g); Cholesterol 0 mg; Sodium 240 mg; Carbohydrate 52 g; (Dietary Fiber 8 g); Protein 11 g; *% Daily Value:* Vitamin A 22%; Vitamin C 92%; Calcium 10%; Iron 28%

Lentil Salad

Lentils are a wonderful source of soluble fiber, and while most people are familiar with the common green lentils, many don't know that they also come in other colors, including white and orange. For a bit more zip, stir 1/4 teaspoon crushed red pepper into the salad.

¹/₂ cup uncooked dried lentils
2 cups chicken broth
Creamy Tomato Dressing (below)
1 cup chopped red bell pepper (about
    1 medium)
¹/₂ cup chopped tomato (about 1 small)
¹/₃ cup chopped green onion (about
    3 medium)
¹/₄ cup chopped red onion

Cover and cook lentils and broth in 2-quart saucepan over medium-low heat 25 minutes or until lentils are tender; drain. Prepare Creamy Tomato Dressing in large glass or plastic bowl. Mix in lentils and remaining ingredients. Cover and refrigerate about 2 hours or until chilled.

2 servings

Creamy Tomato Dressing

¹/₄ cup plain lowfat yogurt
¹/₄ cup tomato juice
3 tablespoons chopped fresh parsley
2 tablespoons red wine vinegar
¹/₂ teaspoon salt
¹/₄ teaspoon pepper

Mix all ingredients.

SERVING SIZE: 1 Serving 95 Calories (10 Calories from Fat); Fat 1 g (Saturated 0 g); Cholesterol 0 mg; Sodium 480 mg; Carbohydrate 14 g; (Dietary Fiber 3 g); Protein 7 g; *% Daily Value:* Vitamin A 12%; Vitamin C 68%; Calcium 4%; Iron 12%

Quinoa Primavera Salad

Quinoa (pronounced "KEEN-wa") was the staple grain of the Inca Indians in Peru. A small grain with a soft crunch, it can be used in any recipe that calls for rice. Be sure to rinse well before using to remove the bitter-tasting, naturally occurring saponin (nature's insect repellent) that forms on the outside of the kernel.

10 sun-dried tomatoes (not oil-packed)
1 can (14$\frac{1}{2}$ ounces) ready-to-serve vegetable broth
1 cup uncooked quinoa
1 cup frozen green peas
1 can (15 to 16 ounces) pinto beans, rinsed and drained
2 teaspoons vegetable oil
$\frac{1}{2}$ cup sliced carrot (about 1 medium)
2 cups sliced zucchini (about 1 medium)
1 small leek, thinly sliced
1 clove garlic, finely chopped
1 tablespoon chopped fresh or 1 teaspoon dried dill weed
3 tablespoons lemon juice
1 tablespoon olive or vegetable oil

Pour enough hot water over sun-dried tomatoes to cover. Let stand 10 to 15 minutes or until softened; drain and cut into halves. Heat broth to boiling in 2-quart saucepan. Stir in quinoa. Heat to boiling; reduce heat to medium. Cover and simmer 10 to 15 minutes or until liquid is absorbed. Mix quinoa, peas, beans and tomatoes in glass or plastic bowl.

Heat 2 teaspoons vegetable oil in 10-inch skillet over medium-high heat. Cook carrot, zucchini, leek and garlic in oil about 8 minutes, stirring frequently, until carrot is crisp-tender. Stir zucchini mixture into quinoa mixture. Mix dill weed, lemon juice and 1 tablespoon olive oil; toss with quinoa mixture. Cover and refrigerate at least 1 hour.

4 servings

SERVING SIZE: 1 Serving 365 Calories (80 Calories from Fat); Fat 9 g (Saturated 1 g); Cholesterol 0 mg; Sodium 360 mg; Carbohydrate 59 g; (Dietary Fiber 4 g); Protein 16 g; *% Daily Value:* Vitamin A 100%; Vitamin C 26%; Calcium 10%; Iron 36%

Quinoa Primavera Salad

Lentil and Wild Rice Salad

Several colors of lentils are available today, from the more familiar grayish-green to white, yellow, red and black. Pick the color you like best!

1/2 cup dried lentils
1 cup water
1/3 cup uncooked wild rice
1 cup water
Cumin Dressing (below)
1/2 cup coarsely shredded carrot (about 1 small)
1/4 cup sliced green onions (2 to 3 medium)
1/4 cup chopped fresh parsley
1/4 cup chopped fresh cilantro leaves

Heat lentils and 1 cup water to boiling; reduce heat. Cover and simmer 25 to 30 minutes or until lentils are tender but not mushy. Rinse wild rice. Heat wild rice and 1 cup water to boiling; reduce heat. Cover and simmer 40 to 50 minutes or until wild rice is tender; cool slightly. Toss lentils, wild rice and remaining ingredients in glass or plastic bowl. Cover and refrigerate about 2 hours or until chilled. Garnish with carrot curls if desired.   **4 servings**

Cumin Dressing

3 tablespoons olive or vegetable oil
1 tablespoon lemon juice
1 teaspoon ground cumin
1/2 teaspoon salt
1/8 teaspoon red pepper sauce
1 clove garlic, crushed

Shake all ingredients in tightly covered container.

SERVING SIZE: 1 Serving 245 Calories (100 Calories from Fat); Fat 11 g (Saturated 1 g); Cholesterol 0 mg; Sodium 280 mg; Carbohydrate 28 g; (Dietary Fiber 5 g); Protein 9 g; *% Daily Value:* Vitamin A 26%; Vitamin C 24%; Calcium 4%; Iron 20%

Southwestern Wild Rice Salad

With this salad, you can have your bowl and eat it too! Large, hollowed-out kaiser rolls hold a zesty wild rice and bean filling that just may "bowl" you over!

1 cup cooked wild or brown rice
1 cup cooked brown or regular long grain rice
3 tablespoons chopped fresh cilantro
1 can (15 to 16 ounces) pinto beans, rinsed and drained
1 can (11 ounces) whole kernel corn with red and green peppers, drained
1 can (4 ounces) chopped green chilies, drained
3 tablespoons white wine vinegar
1 tablespoon Dijon mustard
1/4 teaspoon ground cumin
1/4 teaspoon pepper
4 large kaiser rolls
1/2 cup shredded part-skim mozzarella cheese

Mix wild rice, brown rice, cilantro, beans, corn and chilies. Mix vinegar, mustard, cumin and pepper; toss with rice mixture. Cut 1/2-inch slice from tops of rolls. Remove soft bread from inside of each roll to within 1/2 inch of edge. Reserve bread trimmings for another use. Spoon rice mixture into rolls. Sprinkle with cheese.   **4 servings**

SERVING SIZE: 1 Serving 525 Calories (55 Calories from Fat); Fat 6 g (Saturated 2 g); Cholesterol 10 mg; Sodium 1610 mg; Carbohydrate 107 g; (Dietary Fiber 14 g); Protein 25 g; *% Daily Value:* Vitamin A 6%; Vitamin C 54%; Calcium 20%; Iron 34%

Layered Mexican Salad

1 cup shredded iceberg lettuce
$^1/_4$ cup chopped green bell pepper
1$^1/_4$ cups Black Bean Relish (right)
$^1/_2$ cup whole kernel corn
1 small avocado, peeled and sliced
Lime Vinaigrette (below)

Layer lettuce, bell pepper, $^3/_4$ cup of the Black Bean Relish and the corn in medium bowl. Arrange remaining $^1/_2$ cup relish and the avocado slices on top. Serve with Lime Vinaigrette.

6 servings

Lime Vinaigrette

$^1/_2$ teaspoon grated lime peel
2 tablespoons lime juice
1 tablespoon snipped fresh cilantro
$^1/_4$ teaspoon salt
1 small clove garlic, crushed
$^1/_2$ cup olive oil

Place all ingredients except oil in food processor workbowl fitted with steel blade or in blender container; cover and process until mixed. Gradually pour in oil, processing until thick.

Black Bean Relish

1 can (15 ounces) black beans, rinsed and drained
1 medium tomato, finely chopped (about $^3/_4$ cup)
1 serrano chili, seeded and finely chopped
$^1/_2$ cup chopped red bell pepper
$^1/_4$ cup finely chopped red onion
2 tablespoons white wine vinegar
1 tablespoon vegetable oil
$^1/_4$ teaspoon salt

Mix all ingredients. Cover and refrigerate until chilled, about 1 hour.

2$^1/_2$ cups

SERVING SIZE: 1 Serving 280 Calories (215 Calories from Fat); Fat 24 g (Saturated 4 g); Cholesterol 0 mg; Sodium 220 mg; Carbohydrate 16 g; (Dietary Fiber 4 g); Protein 4 g; *% Daily Value:* Vitamin A 8%; Vitamin C 42%; Calcium 2%; Iron 8%

Spanish Rice Salad

1 tablespoon olive or vegetable oil
$1/2$ cup finely chopped red onion (about
   $1/2$ medium)
1 clove garlic, crushed
$1^1/2$ cups uncooked brown rice
$1/4$ teaspoon ground turmeric
$1/4$ teaspoon crushed red pepper
4 cups Vegetable Stock* (right)
1 cup cooked fresh or frozen peas
$1/2$ cup sliced ripe olives
$1/2$ cup chopped red bell pepper (about
   1 small)
1 medium tomato, cut into wedges
1 can (15 ounces) garbanzo beans,
   drained
1 can (about 15 ounces) artichoke hearts,
   drained and cut into eighths
$1/2$ cup spicy tomato juice or tomato juice
2 tablespoons lemon juice
Lemon wedges, if desired

Heat oil in 2-quart saucepan over medium heat. Cook onion and garlic in oil 2 to 3 minutes, stirring frequently, until onion begins to soften. Stir in rice, turmeric and red pepper; stir to coat rice with oil. Stir in Vegetable Stock. Heat to boiling; reduce heat. Cover and simmer 45 to 50 minutes or until rice is tender.

Carefully mix rice mixture and remaining ingredients except tomato juice, lemon juice and lemon wedges in large bowl. Pour tomato and lemon juices over rice mixture; toss. Cover and refrigerate about 3 hours or until chilled. Serve with lemon wedges. **6 servings**

4 cups hot water and 1 tablespoon plus 1 teaspoon vegetable or chicken bouillon granules can be substituted for the Vegetable Stock.

Vegetable Stock

6 cup coarsely chopped mild vegetables
   (bell peppers, carrots, celery, leeks,
   mushroom stems, potatoes, spinach,
   zucchini)
$1/2$ cup coarsely chopped onion (about
   1 medium)
$1/2$ cup parsley sprigs
8 cups cold water
2 tablespoons chopped fresh or
   2 teaspoons dried basil leaves
2 tablespoons chopped fresh or
   2 teaspoons dried thyme leaves
1 teaspoon salt
$1/4$ teaspoon cracked black pepper
4 cloves garlic, chopped
2 bay leaves

Heat all ingredients to boiling in Dutch oven or stockpot; reduce heat. Cover and simmer about 1 hour, stirring occasionally. Cool slightly. Strain and refrigerate. Stir before measuring.
About 8 cups stock

NOTE: Use strong vegetables, such as broccoli, cabbage, cauliflower, turnips and rutabagas sparingly combined with mild vegetables.

SERVING SIZE: 1 Serving 425 Calories (65 Calories from Fat); Fat 7 g (Saturated 1 g); Cholesterol 0 mg; Sodium 630 mg; Carbohydrate 76 g; (Dietary Fiber 12 g); Protein 15 g; *% Daily Value:* Vitamin A 30%; Vitamin C 82%; Calcium 14%; Iron 32%

Tex-Mex Egg Salad

This very special egg salad turns the ho-hum into the highly delicious!

4 hard-cooked eggs, chopped
¼ cup reduced-calorie mayonnaise or salad dressing
¼ cup low-fat sour cream
¼ cup diced Monterey Jack cheese (1 ounce)
2 tablespoons chopped green onion, with top (about 1 medium)
2 teaspoons chopped fresh cilantro or parsley
¼ teaspoon salt
1 jalapeño chili, seeded and finely chopped
4 medium tomatoes

Mix all ingredients except tomatoes. Cut stem ends from tomatoes. Place tomatoes cut sides down. Cut into sixths to within ½ inch of bottom. Carefully spread out sections. Spoon about ½ cup salad into each tomato.

SERVING SIZE: 1 Serving 195 Calories (115 Calories from Fat); Fat 13 g (Saturated 5 g); Cholesterol 230 mg; Sodium 370 mg; Carbohydrate 11 g; (Dietary Fiber 1 g); Protein 10 g; *% Daily Value:* Vitamin A 30%; Vitamin C 76%; Calcium 10%; Iron 8%

Vegetable-Couscous Salad

This bountiful salad is very quick and easy to prepare and tastes wonderful either slightly warm or at room temperature.

1½ cups uncooked couscous
2 cups boiling water
¼ teaspoon salt
1 can (8 ounces) garbanzo beans (rinsed and drained)
¾ cup chopped seeded tomato (about 1 medium)
½ cup pesto
3 tablespoons lemon juice
⅛ teaspoon pepper
2 green onions, thinly sliced
1 can (15 to 16 ounces) kidney beans, rinsed and drained
4 cups cooked broccoli spears (about 1 pound)

Place couscous in medium bowl. Add boiling water and salt; stir well. Cover and let stand 5 to 7 minutes or until water is absorbed. Stir in remaining ingredients except broccoli. Serve over broccoli. **6 servings**

SERVING SIZE: 1 Serving 380 Calories (80 Calories from Fat); Fat 9 g (Saturated 2 g); Cholesterol 2 mg; Sodium 720 mg; Carbohydrate 69 g; (Dietary Fiber 13 g); Protein 19 g; *% Daily Value:* Vitamin A 24%; Vitamin C 96%; Calcium 16%; Iron 26%

Minted Cottage Cheese Salad with Fruit

Minted Cottage Cheese Salad with Fruit

1 container (16 ounces) small curd
  creamed cottage cheese
1 tablespoon snipped fresh mint leaves
Lettuce leaves
1 cup blueberries, raspberries or
  blackberries
$1/2$ pint medium strawberries (about 1 cup)
  or 1 large peach or nectarine, sliced
2 medium bananas, sliced
Coarsely chopped salted or toasted nuts
Ginger-Honey Dressing (below)

Mix cottage cheese and mint. Divide lettuce leaves among 4 salad plates. Spoon cheese mixture onto each. Arrange fruit on top; sprinkle with nuts. Serve with Ginger-Honey Dressing.

4 servings

Ginger-Honey Dressing

$1/4$ cup vegetable oil
$1/4$ cup lime juice
$1/4$ cup honey
2 tablespoons mayonnaise or salad
  dressing
$1/4$ teaspoon salt
$1/4$ teaspoon ground ginger

Shake all ingredients in tightly covered container.

SERVING SIZE: 1 Serving 500 Calories (260 Calories from Fat); Fat 29 g (Saturated 7 g); Cholesterol 20 mg; Sodium 680 mg; Carbohydrate 45 g; (Dietary Fiber 3 g); Protein 18 g; % *Daily Value:* Vitamin A 8%; Vitamin C 64%; Calcium 10%; Iron 6%

Crunchy Jicama and Melon Salad

$1^1/2$ cups julienne strips jicama (about
  $1/2$ medium)
$1^1/2$ cups $1/2$-inch cubes cantaloupe (about
  $1/2$ medium)
2 tablespoons lime juice
2 tablespoons chopped fresh or 1 tablespoon dried mint leaves
1 teaspoon grated lime peel
1 teaspoon honey
$1/2$ teaspoon salt

Mix all ingredients in glass or plastic bowl. Cover and refrigerate about 2 hours or until chilled.

6 servings

SERVING SIZE: 1 Serving 35 Calories (0 Calories from Fat); Fat 0 g (Saturated 0 g); Cholesterol 0 mg; Sodium 95 mg; Carbohydrate 8 g; (Dietary Fiber 1 g); Protein 1 g; % *Daily Value:* Vitamin A 10%; Vitamin C 42%; Calcium *%; Iron 2%

Seafood Pasta Salad with Ginger Dressing (page 68)

4

Seafood Salads

Smoked Fish Salad

You can buy smoked whitefish or salmon at your supermarket, favorite deli or local fish market.

2 pounds new potatoes (about 16 small)
2 cartons (6 ounces each) lemon yogurt
(about 1¹/₃ cups)
1 jar (2 ounces) diced pimientos, drained
2 teaspoons chopped fresh or ¹/₂ teaspoon
dried dill weed
1 teaspoon dry mustard
¹/₄ teaspoon salt
2 pounds smoked whitefish or salmon
3 medium tomatoes, sliced
1 medium onion, thinly sliced
Salad greens

Heat 1 inch water (salted, if desired) to boiling. Add potatoes. Cover and heat to boiling; reduce heat. Boil 20 to 25 minutes or until tender; drain and allow to cool. Cut into ¹/₄-inch slices. Mix yogurt, pimientos, dill weed, mustard and salt in large bowl. Add potatoes and toss. Cover and refrigerate at least 3 hours.

Remove skin and bones from fish. Divide fish into serving pieces. Arrange potato mixture, fish, tomatoes and onion on salad greens. Garnish with fresh dill weed, if desired.   **8 servings**

SERVING SIZE: 1 Serving 280 Calories (20 Calories from Fat); Fat 2 g (Saturated 1 g); Cholesterol 90 mg; Sodium 970 mg; Carbohydrate 35 g; (Dietary Fiber 2 g); Protein 33 g; *% Daily Value:* Vitamin A 10%; Vitamin C 24%; Calcium 14%; Iron 18%

Safety of Salads in Summer

Any salad mixed with mayonnaise or eggs, so popular for picnics and other large gatherings, deserves special care for safety's sake. Keep these salads cold BEFORE serving, WHEN serving and AFTER serving. Pack them in insulated ice buckets or coolers. Serve them in larger bowls full of ice cubes, and keep them in the shade. Then chill any leftover salad immediately to use within 48 hours.

Cod Salad with Thai Sauce

A daikon is a large white radish with a mild flavor. It's used here to balance the bite of the red radish. If red radishes don't agree with you, replace them with thinly sliced carrots or chopped apple.

    Thai Sauce (below)
    3 cups shredded lettuce (about 1 small
        head)
    3 cups 1-inch pieces cooked cod or
        whitefish (about 1½ pounds)
    1 cup sliced red radishes (about
        12 medium)
    1 cup sliced daikon white radish (about
        1 medium)
    1 tablespoon chopped fresh cilantro
        leaves
    1 tablespoon flaked coconut

Prepare Thai Sauce. Divide lettuce among 6 plates. Top with fish and radishes. Sprinkle with cilantro and coconut. Serve with sauce.

6 servings

Thai Sauce

    ½ cup chicken broth
    2 tablespoons lime juice
    1 teaspoon chopped fresh or ¼ teaspoon
        dried mint leaves
    1 teaspoon chopped fresh or ¼ teaspoon
        dried basil leaves
    1 teaspoon finely chopped fresh
        gingerroot
    1 teaspoon finely chopped hot chili
    2 teaspoons reduced-sodium soy sauce

Mix all ingredients.

SERVING SIZE: 1 Serving 100 Calories (20 Calories from Fat); Fat 2 g (Saturated 1 g); Cholesterol 45 mg; Sodium 220 mg; Carbohydrate 3 g; (Dietary Fiber 1 g); Protein 17 g; *% Daily Value:* Vitamin A 2%; Vitamin C 22%; Calcium 2%; Iron 4%

Warm Mahimahi Salad

You can substitute cod, halibut or scrod for the mahimahi, if you like.

    ⅓ cup thinly sliced green onions
    ½ cup orange juice
    2 tablespoons lemon juice
    1 teaspoon finely chopped gingerroot
    2 teaspoons reduced-sodium soy sauce
    ¼ teaspoon pepper
    1½ pounds mahimahi fillets, skinned, cut
        into 6 serving pieces
    6 cups bite-size pieces spinach
    3 medium oranges, peeled and thinly
        sliced
    1 small cucumber, sliced
    1 tablespoon vegetable oil

Mix onions, orange juice, lemon juice, gingerroot, soy sauce and pepper in shallow glass or plastic dish. Add fish fillets; turn to coat with marinade. Cover and refrigerate at least 2 hours.

Set oven control to broil. Spray broiler pan rack with nonstick cooking spray. Remove fish from marinade; reserve marinade. Place fish on rack in broiler pan. Broil with tops about 4 inches from heat 4 minutes; turn. Broil 5 to 7 minutes longer or until fish flakes easily with fork. Arrange spinach, oranges and cucumber on dinner plates. Place fish on spinach mixture. Pour marinade and oil into 1-quart saucepan. Boil until reduced to ½ cup. Pour over fish.   **6 servings**

SERVING SIZE: 1 Serving 140 Calories (20 Calories from Fat); Fat 2 g (Saturated 0 g); Cholesterol 60 mg; Sodium 240 mg; Carbohydrate 6 g; (Dietary Fiber 3 g); Protein 25 g; *% Daily Value:* Vitamin A 80%; Vitamin C 24%; Calcium 12%; Iron 18%

Seafood Salad with Dill Dressing

Creamy Dill Dressing (below)
1¹/₂ cups cooked medium shrimp (about ¹/₂ pound shelled)*
1 cup cut-up cooked crabmeat**
¹/₄ cup sliced green onions (with tops)
1 medium cucumber, chopped
1 can (8¹/₂ ounces) sliced water chestnuts, drained
2 avocados, peeled and sliced
Salad greens

Prepare Creamy Dill Dressing; toss with remaining ingredients except avocados and salad greens. Cover and refrigerate at least 1 hour.

Arrange avocados on salad greens. Top with shrimp mixture. **4 or 5 servings**

*1 package (6 ounces) frozen cooked medium shrimp, thawed, or 2 cans (4¹/₂ ounces each) large shrimp, drained, can be substituted for the fresh shrimp.

**1 package (6 ounces) frozen cooked crabmeat, thawed, drained and cartilage removed, can be substituted for the fresh crabmeat.

Head Start Salad Dressings

For Vegetable Salads: Add extra zest to homemade salads with these dressing ideas.
- ¹/₄ cup oil and vinegar salad dressing and ¹/₄ teaspoon chili powder
- ¹/₄ cup oil and vinegar salad dressing and ¹/₄ teaspoon dried oregano leaves
- ¹/₄ cup oil and vinegar salad dressing and ¹/₄ teaspoon ground savory
- ¹/₄ cup oil and vinegar salad dressing and ¹/₄ teaspoon dried thyme leaves
- ¹/₄ cup of mayonnaise or salad dressing and ¹/₄ cup catsup
- ¹/₂ cup of mayonnaise or salad dressing and ¹/₄ cup chili sauce, 1 drop red pepper sauce and dash of chili powder
- ¹/₂ cup of mayonnaise or salad dressing and ¹/₄ cup frozen whipped topping (thawed)

Creamy Dill Dressing

¹/₂ cup mayonnaise or salad dressing
¹/₄ cup sour cream or plain yogurt
2 tablespoons lemon juice
1 teaspoon snipped fresh dill weed or ¹/₄ teaspoon dried dill weed
¹/₄ teaspoon salt

Mix all ingredients.

SERVING SIZE: 1 Serving 470 Calories (350 Calories from Fat); Fat 39 g (Saturated 8 g); Cholesterol 140 mg; Sodium 500 mg; Carbohydrate 17 g; (Dietary Fiber 6 g); Protein 19 g; *% Daily Value:* Vitamin A 16%; Vitamin C 34%; Calcium 10%; Iron 18%

Tuna-Couscous Salad

1 cup uncooked couscous
¼ cup sliced green onions with tops (about 2 medium)
2 cans (6½ ounces each) solid white tuna in water, drained
1 package (9 ounces) frozen cut green beans, thawed and drained
1 can (8 ounces) sliced water chestnuts, drained
½ cup reduced-calorie mayonnaise or salad dressing
½ cup plain nonfat yogurt
2 tablespoons cider vinegar
2 tablespoons chopped fresh or 2 teaspoons dried basil leaves
¼ teaspoon salt
3 cups bite-size pieces greens (spinach, leaf lettuce, romaine)
1 large tomato, cut into 12 wedges

Cook couscous as directed on package—except omit salt and margarine. Mix couscous, onions, tuna, green beans and water chestnuts in medium bowl. Mix remaining ingredients except greens and tomato wedges in separate bowl. Stir into couscous mixture. Cover and refrigerate about 3 hours or until chilled. Serve on greens; garnish with tomato wedges. **6 servings**

SERVING SIZE: 1 Serving 280 Calories (65 Calories from Fat); Fat 7 g (Saturated 1 g); Cholesterol 20 mg; Sodium 440 mg; Carbohydrate 37 g; (Dietary Fiber 4 g); Protein 21 g; *% Daily Value:* Vitamin A 6%; Vitamin C 22%; Calcium 8%; Iron 12%

Tuna and Tomato Salad

¼ cup olive or vegetable oil
¼ cup wine vinegar
½ teaspoon red pepper sauce
2 medium tomatoes, coarsely chopped
1 bunch green onions (with tops), sliced
1 clove garlic, crushed
1 can (9¼ ounces) tuna, drained
½ pound fresh asparagus, cut diagonally into 1-inch pieces*
6 cups bite-size pieces salad greens
Freshly ground pepper

Mix oil, vinegar, pepper sauce, tomatoes, onions, garlic and tuna in 4-quart bowl. Layer asparagus and salad greens on tuna mixture. Cover and refrigerate at least 2 hours but no longer than 24 hours. Sprinkle with pepper and toss just before serving. **4 servings**

2 cups chopped broccoli can be substituted for the asparagus.

SERVING SIZE: 1 Serving 230 Calories (135 Calories from Fat); Fat 15 g (Saturated 2 g); Cholesterol 15 mg; Sodium 220 mg; Carbohydrate 9 g; (Dietary Fiber 2 g); Protein 17 g; *% Daily Value:* Vitamin A 10%; Vitamin C 46%; Calcium 6%; Iron 12%

Fresh Tuna and Red Potato Salad

Mix the ingredients while the potatoes are still hot—their warmth releases the flavors of the dressing, allowing the potatoes to absorb more flavor. In fact, if the potatoes and tuna are both hot, you can eat this immediately as a warm salad.

3 cups $\frac{1}{2}$-inch cubes cooked red potatoes (about 1 pound)
3 cups 1-inch pieces grilled yellowfin tuna or other lean fish fillets (about 1 pound)
2 cups chopped celery (about 4 medium stalks)
1 cup plain nonfat yogurt
$\frac{1}{4}$ cup chopped fresh parsley
2 tablespoons red wine vinegar or cider vinegar
$\frac{1}{2}$ teaspoon salt
$\frac{1}{2}$ teaspoon ground cumin
$\frac{1}{4}$ teaspoon pepper

Mix all ingredients in glass or plastic bowl. Cover and refrigerate about 2 hours, or until chilled.

6 servings

SERVING SIZE: 1 Serving 185 Calories (25 Calories from Fat); Fat 3 g (Saturated 1 g); Cholesterol 45 mg; Sodium 270 mg; Carbohydrate 20 g; (Dietary Fiber 2 g); Protein 20 g; *% Daily Value:* Vitamin A 2%; Vitamin C 12%; Calcium 16%; Iron 12%

Italian Tuna and Spiral Pasta Salad

1 package (7 ounces) uncooked spiral macaroni (about 3 cups)
2 cans ($6\frac{1}{2}$ ounces each) tuna, chilled and drained
1 jar (6 ounces) marinated artichoke hearts, chilled and undrained
$\frac{1}{4}$ cup Italian dressing
2 tablespoons snipped parsley
2 tablespoons capers, drained
Dash of pepper

Cook macaroni as directed on package; drain. Rinse in cold water; drain. Mix macaroni and remaining ingredients. Serve on salad greens, if desired.

4 servings

SERVING SIZE: 1 Serving 375 Calories (90 Calories from Fat); Fat 10 g (Saturated 2 g); Cholesterol 25 mg; Sodium 500 mg; Carbohydrate 44 g; (Dietary Fiber 2 g); Protein 29 g; *% Daily Value:* Vitamin A 2%; Vitamin C 10%; Calcium 4%; Iron 20%

Seafood Pasta Salad with Ginger Dressing

8 ounces uncooked vermicelli
Ginger Dressing (below)
2 cups bite-size pieces cooked seafood or
   1 package (8 ounces) frozen salad-style
   imitation crabmeat, thawed
1/2 cup coarsely chopped jicama or water
   chestnuts
1/4 cup snipped cilantro or parsley
2 medium carrots, shredded
1 medium cucumber, halved and sliced

Break vermicelli into halves. Cook as directed on package; drain. Rinse in cold water; drain.

Prepare Ginger Dressing. Toss dressing, vermicelli and remaining ingredients. Spoon onto salad greens, if desired.   **6 servings**

Ginger Dressing

1/3 cup mayonnaise or salad dressing
1/3 cup plain yogurt
1 tablespoon soy sauce
1 teaspoon sugar
1/2 teaspoon ground ginger
Dash of red pepper sauce, hot chili oil or
   hot sesame oil

Mix all ingredients in large bowl.

SERVING SIZE: 1 Serving 305 Calories (100 Calories from Fat); Fat 11 g (Saturated 2 g); Cholesterol 20 mg; Sodium 640 mg; Carbohydrate 40 g; (Dietary Fiber 2 g); Protein 13 g; *% Daily Value:* Vitamin A 40%; Vitamin C 10%; Calcium 4%; Iron 10%

Seafood Salad with Tomato-Mint Vinaigrette

You can serve this salad different ways. For dinner, try it with a whole wheat roll. For lunch, toss the spinach in with the salad and stuff into pitas.

Tomato-Mint Vinaigrette (below)
3 cups cooked broccoli flowerets (1 large
   bunch)
1 cup cooked bay scallops
1 cup 1 1/2-inch pieces cooked salmon
1 cup 1 1/2-inch pieces cooked whitefish
3 cups shredded spinach (about 4 ounces)

Prepare Tomato-Mint Vinaigrette. Toss with broccoli, scallops, salmon and whitefish. Serve over spinach.   **6 servings**

Tomato-Mint Vinaigrette

1/2 cup chopped roma (plum) tomatoes
   (about 2 medium)
1/3 cup finely chopped red onion (about
   1/2 small)
1/2 cup chicken broth
2 tablespoons chopped fresh or
   2 teaspoons dried mint leaves
2 tablespoons cider vinegar
1 tablespoon chopped sun-dried tomatoes
   (not oil-packed)
1 tablespoon apple juice
1/4 teaspoon salt
1/4 teaspoon pepper
1 clove garlic, finely chopped

Mix all ingredients. Cover and refrigerate 1 hour.

SERVING SIZE: 1 Serving 145 Calories (25 Calories from Fat); Fat 3 g (Saturated 1 g); Cholesterol 35 mg; Sodium 280 mg; Carbohydrate 9 g; (Dietary Fiber 4 g); Protein 21 g; *% Daily Value:* Vitamin A 44%; Vitamin C 84%; Calcium 14%; Iron 16%

Marinated Herbed Salmon

If fresh salmon is not available, try substituting 1 can (15 1/2 ounces) salmon, drained.

1 teaspoon salt
1/4 teaspoon dried dill weed
3 slices lemon
2 salmon steaks, each about 1-inch thick
1 small onion, thinly sliced
1/4 cup wine vinegar
1/4 teaspoon dried tarragon leaves
1 small cucumber
1/2 cup plain yogurt
1/4 teaspoon salt
1/8 teaspoon dried dill weed
Lettuce leaves
2 medium tomatoes, sliced

Heat 1 inch water, 1 teaspoon salt, 1/4 teaspoon dill weed and lemon slices to boiling in 10-inch skillet; reduce heat. Arrange salmon steaks in skillet. Simmer uncovered until salmon flakes easily with fork, 6 to 8 minutes; drain. Carefully remove skin from salmon.

Place salmon in shallow glass or plastic dish; arrange onion on salmon. Mix vinegar and tarragon; drizzle over onion and salmon. Cover and refrigerate at least 8 hours but no longer than 24 hours.

About 20 minutes before serving, cut cucumber lengthwise into halves; remove seeds. Cut halves crosswise into thin slices. Mix cucumber, yogurt, 1/4 teaspoon salt and 1/8 teaspoon dill weed.

Place salmon on lettuce leaves; arrange onion and tomatoes around salmon. Drizzle any remaining marinade over salmon. Serve with cucumber mixture. Garnish with fresh dill weed, if desired. **4 servings**

SERVING SIZE: 1 Serving 245 Calories (80 Calories from Fat); Fat 9 g (Saturated 3 g); Cholesterol 95 mg; Sodium 780 mg; Carbohydrate 9 g; (Dietary Fiber 1 g); Protein 33 g; *% Daily Value:* Vitamin A 12%; Vitamin C 38%; Calcium 8%; Iron 8%

Salmon-Pasta Salad with Spinach Pesto

Spinach is used in place of the traditional fresh basil for a colorful and dish full of flavor.

Spinach Pesto (below)
3 cups 1 1/2-inch pieces cooked salmon or other fatty fish fillets (about 1 pound)
3 cups cooked ziti pasta
2 cups cooked cut green beans (about 11 ounces)
2 cups shredded zucchini (about 2 medium)
2 cups chopped roma (plum) tomatoes (about 8 medium)
1 cup cooked fresh, frozen (thawed) or canned (drained) whole kernel corn (about 2 medium ears)

Prepare Spinach Pesto. Mix pesto and remaining ingredients in large glass or plastic bowl. Cover and refrigerate at least 2 hours.

6 servings

Spinach Pesto

1 cup fresh parsley sprigs
3/4 cup cooked chopped spinach
1/2 cup chicken broth
2 tablespoons lemon juice
1 teaspoon olive or vegetable oil
1/4 teaspoon salt
1/4 teaspoon pepper
1 garlic clove, cut into halves

Place all ingredients in blender or food processor. Cover and blend on high 30 seconds or until smooth.

SERVING SIZE: 1 Serving 280 Calories (55 Calories from Fat); Fat 6 g (Saturated 1 g); Cholesterol 30 mg; Sodium 330 mg; Carbohydrate 33 g; (Dietary Fiber 4 g); Protein 23 g; *% Daily Value:* Vitamin A 32%; Vitamin C 64%; Calcium 10%; Iron 18%

Salmon-Rice Salad with Dilled Cucumber Dressing

Winter cucumbers sometimes grow a thick, almost bitter skin. If that is the case, run the tines of a fork down the length of a peeled cucumber scoring deeply into the pale flesh. You'll still be able to enjoy the pale green color (and fiber, too).

Dilled Cucumber Dressing (below)
2 medium cucumbers, thinly sliced
1 pound salmon steaks*, poached, chilled
    and flaked
1 cup cold cooked wild rice
1/2 cup cold cooked white rice
1/4 cup sliced green onions (with tops)
12 cherry tomatoes, cut into halves

Prepare Dilled Cucumber Dressing. Arrange cucumber slices, overlapping edges, in circle on each of 4 plates. Toss remaining ingredients; spoon into center of cucumbers. Spoon Dilled Cucumber Dressing over salads. **4 servings, about 1 cup salmon mixture and 1/3 cup dressing each**

1 can (15 1/2 ounces) salmon, drained and flaked, can be substituted for the salmon steaks.

Dilled Cucumber Dressing

1 cup plain nonfat yogurt
1/2 cup chopped seeded cucumber
2 tablespoons reduced-calorie mayon-
    naise or salad dressing
1 tablespoon snipped fresh dill weed or
    1 teaspoon dried dill weed
1/2 teaspoon celery salt
1/2 teaspoon onion powder

Place all ingredients in blender container. Cover and blend on high speed until smooth, about 15 seconds. Cover and refrigerate until chilled, at least 2 hours.

SERVING SIZE: 1 Serving 315 Calories (90 Calories from Fat); Fat 10 g (Saturated 3 g); Cholesterol 80 mg; Sodium 360 mg; Carbohydrate 26 g; (Dietary Fiber 1 g); Protein 31 g; *% Daily Value:* Vitamin A 10%; Vitamin C 32%; Calcium 16%; Iron 10%

Grilled Salmon Salad

4 small salmon steaks, each about 1-inch
    thick (about 1 1/2 pounds)
1 tablespoon snipped fresh marjoram
    leaves or 1 teaspoon dried marjoram
    leaves
1/2 teaspoon salt
1/4 teaspoon pepper
1/2 cup oil-and-vinegar dressing
6 cups mixed salad greens
2 tablespoons capers, drained

Sprinkle salmon steaks with marjoram, salt and pepper. Set oven control to broil. Place salmon on rack in broiler pan; drizzle with 1 tablespoon of the dressing.

Broil salmon with tops about 3 inches from heat until opaque, 7 to 10 minutes. Turn; drizzle with 1 tablespoon dressing. Broil until salmon flakes easily with fork, about 5 minutes longer.

Mix salad greens and capers; toss with remaining dressing. Divide among 4 plates; top with salmon steaks. **4 servings**

SERVING SIZE: 1 Serving 380 Calories (215 Calories from Fat); Fat 24 g (Saturated 5 g); Cholesterol 110 mg; Sodium 610 mg; Carbohydrate 5 g; (Dietary Fiber 1 g); Protein 37 g; *% Daily Value:* Vitamin A 8%; Vitamin C 4%; Calcium 4%; Iron 10%

Grilled Salmon Salad

Salmon-Squash Salad

Sesame Dressing (below)
1½ cups thinly sliced zucchini (about
    1 small)
1½ cups thinly sliced yellow summer
    squash (about 1 small)
1 cup sliced celery (about 2 medium
    stalks)
1 small onion, sliced and separated into
    rings
1 cup sliced mushrooms (about 3 ounces)
Lettuce cups or leaves
1 can (15½ ounces) salmon, chilled,
    drained and flaked
12 cherry tomatoes

Prepare Sesame Dressing. Toss zucchini, summer squash, celery, onion and mushrooms. Place lettuce cups on each of 6 salad plates. Spoon vegetable mixture into lettuce cups. Place salmon on center of vegetable mixture. Top each with 2 cherry tomatoes. Spoon Sesame Dressing over salads. **6 servings, about 1 cup each**

Sesame Dressing

1 tablespoon sesame seed
⅓ cup white wine vinegar
1 tablespoon sugar
2 tablespoons olive or vegetable oil
1 teaspoon dry mustard
½ teaspoon salt
1 large clove garlic, crushed

Cook sesame seed over medium heat, stirring frequently, until golden brown; cool. Shake seed and remaining ingredients in tightly covered container. Refrigerate about 2 hours or until chilled. Remove garlic and shake dressing before serving.

SERVING SIZE: 1 Serving 165 Calories (80 Calories from Fat); Fat 9 g (Saturated 2 g); Cholesterol 35 mg; Sodium 540 mg; Carbohydrate 9 g; (Dietary Fiber 2 g); Protein 14 g; *% Daily Value:* Vitamin A 8%; Vitamin C 26%; Calcium 16%; Iron 8%

Scallop and Black Bean Salad

1 pound bay scallops
2 cups cooked black beans or 1 can
    (15 ounces) black beans, rinsed and
    drained
2 cups chopped jicama (about 1 medium)
1 cup chopped green bell pepper (about
    1 medium)
1 cup chopped red bell pepper (about
    1 medium)
1 cup plain nonfat yogurt
½ cup finely chopped red onion (about
    ½ medium)
½ teaspoon salt
½ teaspoon ground coriander

Set oven control to broil. Spray broiler pan rack with nonstick cooking spray. Place scallops on rack in broiler pan. Broil with tops about 4 inches from heat about 5 minutes or until scallops are white.

Mix scallops and remaining ingredients in large glass or plastic bowl. Cover and refrigerate 2 hours. **6 servings**

SERVING SIZE: 1 Serving 230 Calories (20 Calories from Fat); Fat 2 g (Saturated 1 g); Cholesterol 25 mg; Sodium 530 mg; Carbohydrate 28 g; (Dietary Fiber 6 g); Protein 25 g; *% Daily Value:* Vitamin A 12%; Vitamin C 80%; Calcium 22%; Iron 24%

Salmon-Squash Salad

Scallop Seviche

**1 pound sea scallops, cooked and cut into
1-inch pieces
1 cup chopped peeled cucumber (about
1 medium)
1 cup chopped green bell pepper (about
1 medium)
1 cup chopped red bell peppper (about 1
medium)
1 cup finely chopped jicama (about
¹/₂ medium)
1 cup chopped tomato (about 1 large)
³/₄ cup finely chopped red onion (about
1 medium)
¹/₂ cup lime juice
3 tablespoons chopped fresh cilantro
leaves
1 teaspoon vegetable oil
¹/₂ teaspoon salt
¹/₂ teaspoon crushed red pepper
¹/₄ teaspoon pepper
Lettuce leaves**

Mix all ingredients except lettuce leaves in glass or plastic bowl. Cover and refrigerate at least 4 hours. Serve over lettuce leaves.   **6 servings**

SERVING SIZE: 1 Serving 140 Calories (20 Calories from Fat); Fat 2 g (Saturated 0 g); Cholesterol 25 mg; Sodium 390 mg; Carbohydrate 12 g; (Dietary Fiber 2 g); Protein 18 g; % *Daily Value:* Vitamin A 20%; Vitamin C 100%; Calcium 10%; Iron 16%

Salmon Salad with Cucumber Noodles

These fun "noodles" are actually cut from cucumbers. Ordinary cucumbers can be used—just cut in half and remove the seeds.

**Cucumber-Yogurt Sauce (below)
2 English cucumbers, peeled
3 cups 1-inch pieces grilled salmon or
other fatty fish fillets (about 1 pound)
3 cups cooked cut green beans (about
1 pound)
2 cups cherry tomatoes, cut into halves
(about 1 pint)
¹/₄ cup chopped green onions (2 to
3 medium)**

Prepare Cucumber-Yogurt Sauce. Cut cucumbers into thin strips, 8 × ¹/₄ inch, using vegetable peeler. Divide cucumbers, fish, beans and tomatoes among 6 plates. Sprinkle with onions. Serve with sauce.   **6 servings**

Cucumber-Yogurt Sauce

**³/₄ cup plain nonfat yogurt
¹/₂ cup chopped peeled cucumber (about
¹/₂ medium)
2 tablespoons chopped fresh chives
2 tablespoons low-fat sour cream
2 teaspoons Dijon mustard
¹/₂ teaspoon salt
¹/₄ teaspoon pepper**

Mix all ingredients. Cover and refrigerate 1 hour.

SERVING SIZE: 1 Serving 180 Calories (45 Calories from Fat); Fat 5 g (1 Saturated g); Cholesterol 30 mg; Sodium 280 mg; Carbohydrate 14 g; (Dietary Fiber 3 g); Protein 20 g; % *Daily Value:* Vitamin A 10%; Vitamin C 30%; Calcium 14%; Iron 10%

Scallop Seviche

Salad Niçoise

Vinaigrette Dressing (below)
1 package (9 ounces) frozen whole or
Italian-style green beans*
1 head Boston or leaf lettuce, torn into
bite-size pieces
4 Italian plum tomatoes or 2 medium
tomatoes, sliced
2 hard-cooked eggs, cut into fourths
1 can (9¼ ounces) tuna, drained
½ cup Greek or ripe olives
1 can (about 2 ounces) anchovy fillets
Snipped parsley

Prepare Vinaigrette Dressing. Cook beans as directed on package; drain. Cover and refrigerate at least 1 hour.

Place lettuce on salad plates; arrange beans, tomatoes and eggs around edge. Mound tuna in center. Garnish with olives, anchovies and parsley. Serve with dressing. **4 servings**

* *¾ pound fresh green beans, cooked (about 2 cups), can be substituted for the frozen green beans.*

Vinaigrette Dressing

½ cup olive or vegetable oil
¼ cup white wine vinegar
½ teaspoon salt
1½ teaspoons snipped fresh basil leaves
or ½ teaspoon dried basil leaves
¼ teaspoon dry mustard
⅛ teaspoon pepper

Shake all ingredients in tightly covered container; refrigerate.

SERVING SIZE: 1 Serving 425 Calories (295 Calories from Fat); Fat 33 g (Saturated 5 g); Cholesterol 135 mg; Sodium 1080 mg; Carbohydrate 11 g; (Dietary Fiber 3 g); Protein 24 g; % Daily Value: Vitamin A 16%; Vitamin C 42%; Calcium 10%; Iron 20%

Crab Louis

Louis Dressing (below)
4 cups bite-size pieces salad greens
2 cups cut-up cooked crabmeat or
1 package (8 ounces) frozen salad-style
imitation crabmeat, thawed*
4 tomatoes, cut into fourths
4 hard-cooked eggs, cut into fourths
Ripe or pimiento-stuffed olives

Prepare Louis Dressing. Divide salad greens among 4 salad bowls or plates. Arrange crabmeat, tomatoes, eggs and olives on lettuce. Pour Louis Dressing over salads. **4 servings**

2 packages (6 ounces each) frozen cooked crabmeat, thawed and drained, or 2 cans (6½ ounces each) crabmeat, drained and cartilage removed, can be substituted for the cooked or imitation crabmeat.

Louis Dressing

¾ cup chili sauce
½ cup mayonnaise or salad dressing
1 teaspoon finely chopped onion
½ teaspoon sugar
¼ teaspoon Worcestershire sauce
Salt to taste

Mix all ingredients. Refrigerate at least 30 minutes.

SERVING SIZE: 1 Serving 440 Calories (270 Calories from Fat); Fat 30 g (Saturated 5 g); Cholesterol 295 mg; Sodium 1310 mg; Carbohydrate 22 g; (Dietary Fiber 2 g); Protein 22 g; % Daily Value: Vitamin A 24%; Vitamin C 58%; Calcium 12%; Iron 16%

Salad Niçoise with French Potato Salad (page 83)

Marinated Shrimp Kabob Salad

The salad greens can vary from all of one kind to a mixture of several.

- 1 tablespoon grated orange peel
- 1/2 cup orange juice
- 2 tablespoons vegetable oil
- 1/2 teaspoon crushed red pepper
- 1/4 teaspoon salt
- 2 cloves garlic, crushed
- 16 large raw shrimp, peeled and deveined
- 8 ounces jicama, peeled and cut into 1-inch pieces
- 1 medium red bell pepper, cut into 1 1/2-inch pieces
- 1/2 small pineapple, peeled and cut into chunks
- 4 cups bite-size pieces salad greens

Mix orange peel, orange juice, oil, red pepper, salt and garlic in large glass or plastic bowl. Reserve 1/3 cup orange juice mixture; cover and refrigerate. Toss shrimp and remaining orange juice mixture in bowl. Cover and refrigerate at least 2 hours but no longer than 24 hours.

Set oven control to broil. Remove shrimp from marinade; reserve marinade. Thread shrimp, jicama, bell pepper and pineapple alternately on each of eight 10-inch skewers.* Place on rack in broiler pan.

Broil with tops about 4 inches from heat about 8 minutes, turning and brushing once with marinade, until shrimp are pink. Arrange salad greens on 4 plates. Top each with 2 kabobs; remove skewers. Serve with reserved orange juice mixture. **4 servings**

If using bamboo skewers, soak in water at least 30 minutes before using to prevent burning.

SERVING SIZE: 1 Serving 170 Calories (70 Calories from Fat); Fat 8 g (Saturated 2 g); Cholesterol 55 mg; Sodium 200 mg; Carbohydrate 17 g; (Dietary Fiber 2 g); Protein 7 g; *% Daily Value:* Vitamin A 14%; Vitamin C 100%; Calcium 4%; Iron 10%

Tangy Shrimp Noodle Salad

- 2 cups uncooked noodles (about 4 ounces)
- 2 cups coarsely chopped zucchini (about 2 medium)
- 1/2 cup sliced celery (1 medium stalk)
- 1/4 cup sliced ripe olives
- 1 can (4 1/4 ounces) tiny shrimp, rinsed and drained
- Horseradish Dressing (below)
- Salad greens

Cook noodles as directed on package; drain. Mix all ingredients except salad greens. Refrigerate at least 2 hours but no longer than 24 hours. Spoon onto salad greens. **4 servings, about 1 1/2 cups each**

Horseradish Dressing

- 1 cup plain nonfat yogurt
- 1/3 cup reduced-calorie sour cream
- 2 tablespoons prepared horseradish
- 1 tablespoon finely chopped onion

Mix all ingredients.

SERVING SIZE: 1 Serving 210 Calories (35 Calories from Fat); Fat 4 g (Saturated 1 g); Cholesterol 80 mg; Sodium 230 mg; Carbohydrate 31 g; (Dietary Fiber 3 g); Protein 15 g; *% Daily Value:* Vitamin A 10%; Vitamin C 20%; Calcium 20%; Iron 16%

Dilled Egg and Shrimp Salad

1/3 cup mayonnaise or salad dressing
2 teaspoons snipped fresh dill weed or
   1/2 teaspoon dried dill weed
1 teaspoon prepared mustard
1/2 teaspoon salt
1/4 teaspoon pepper
6 hard-cooked eggs, chilled and coarsely
   chopped
2 stalks celery, sliced
2 green onions (with tops), sliced
1 package (6 ounces) frozen cooked
   shrimp, thawed
Lettuce leaves

Mix mayonnaise, dill, mustard, salt and pepper in large bowl until well blended. Gently stir in eggs, celery, onions and shrimp. Serve immediately on lettuce leaves or store in refrigerator.

4 servings

SERVING SIZE: 1 Serving 295 Calories (205 Calories from Fat); Fat 23 g (Saturated 5 g); Cholesterol 410 mg; Sodium 600 mg; Carbohydrate 3 g; (Dietary Fiber 0 g); Protein 19 g; *% Daily Value:* Vitamin A 18%; Vitamin C 12%; Calcium 8%; Iron 16%

South Seas Shrimp Salad

You can make your own five-spice powder by mixing 1 teaspoon ground cinnamon, 1 star anise or 1 teaspoon anise seed, 1 teaspoon fennel seed, 1/4 teaspoon peppercorns and 1/4 teaspoon ground cloves in a blender. Blend on high speed until finely ground. Store powder in a tightly covered container.

2 cups bite-size pieces spinach
2 cups shredded Chinese cabbage
8 ounces cooked cleaned shrimp (about
   1 1/2 cups)
1 cup enoki mushrooms
1/4 cup slivered almonds, toasted
1 red bell pepper, cut into 1/2-inch pieces
1 green onion (with top), thinly sliced
   (about 1 tablespoon)
2 tablespoons vegetable oil
2 tablespoons rice vinegar or vinegar
2 tablespoons soy sauce
1/2 teaspoon five-spice powder

Mix spinach, cabbage, shrimp, mushrooms, almonds, bell pepper and onion. Shake remaining ingredients in tightly covered container. Pour over spinach mixture and toss.

**4 servings,
about 2 cups each**

SERVING SIZE: 1 Serving 195 Calories (115 Calories from Fat); Fat 13 g (Saturated 2 g); Cholesterol 110 mg; Sodium 690 mg; Carbohydrate 7 g; (Dietary Fiber 3 g); Protein 16 g; *% Daily Value:* Vitamin A 48%; Vitamin C 100%; Calcium 10%; Iron 22%

Mexican Flag Salad

5

Fruit and Vegetable Salads

■

Mexican Flag Salad

6 cups water
2 tablespoons lime juice
1 pound whole green beans
1 small jicama, peeled and cut into $1/4$-inch strips (about 2 cups)
2 red bell peppers, cut into $1/4$-inch strips
Herbed Vinaigrette (right)
Lettuce leaves
6 to 8 ripe olives, finely chopped

Heat water and lime juice to boiling. Place green beans in wire strainer; lower into boiling water. Cover and cook 5 minutes. Immediately rinse under running cold water; drain.

Place beans, jicama and bell peppers in separate bowls. Pour $1/4$ cup Herbed Vinaigrette over each vegetable. Cover and refrigerate at least 1 hour.

Arrange beans, jicama and bell peppers on lettuce leaves in Mexican flag design. Place olives in center of rectangle formed by jicama.

6 to 8 servings

Herbed Vinaigrette

$1/2$ cup olive or vegetable oil
2 tablespoons lemon juice
2 tablespoons lime juice
1 tablespoon wine vinegar
1 teaspoon snipped parsley
1 teaspoon chili powder
$1/2$ teaspoon dry mustard
$1/4$ teaspoon salt
$1/4$ teaspoon dried basil leaves
$1/4$ teaspoon dried oregano leaves
$1/4$ teaspoon ground sage
$1/8$ teaspoon freshly ground pepper
1 clove garlic, finely chopped

Shake all ingredients in tightly covered container.

SERVING SIZE: 1 Serving 215 Calories (170 Calories from Fat); Fat 19 g (Saturated 3 g); Cholesterol 0 mg; Sodium 145 mg; Carbohydrate 13 g; (Dietary Fiber 4 g); Protein 2 g; *% Daily Value:* Vitamin A 22%; Vitamin C 100%; Calcium 4%; Iron 8%

Greek Salad

Greek olives and feta cheese make this a classic Greek salad. It would go well with grilled meat.

   1 medium head lettuce, torn into bite-size
      pieces
   1 bunch romaine, torn into bite-size pieces
   24 Greek or green olives
   10 radishes, sliced
   1 medium cucumber, sliced
   1 bunch green onions, cut into $1/2$-inch
      pieces
   1 cup crumbled feta or chèvre (about
      4 ounces)
   1 carrot, shredded
   Vinegar dressing (below)

Toss lettuce and romaine. Arrange remaining ingredients except Vinegar Dressing on top. Serve with dressing.   **6 servings**

Vinegar Dressing

   $1/2$ cup olive or vegetable oil
   $1/3$ cup wine vinegar
   1 tablespoon snipped fresh oregano
      leaves or 1 teaspoon dried oregano
      leaves
   1 teaspoon salt

Shake all ingredients in tightly covered container.

SERVING SIZE: 1 Serving 285 Calories (235 Calories from Fat); Fat 26 g (Saturated 7 g); Cholesterol 20 mg; Sodium 810 mg; Carbohydrate 10 g; (Dietary Fiber 3 g); Protein 6 g; *% Daily Value:* Vitamin A 44%; Vitamin C 44%; Calcium 20%; Iron 14%

Potato Salad

A summer favorite! If you are taking this to a picnic, be sure to keep it in a cooler.

   2 pounds potatoes (about 6 medium),
      peeled
   $1 1/2$ cups mayonnaise or salad dressing
   1 tablespoon white or cider vinegar
   1 tablespoon prepared mustard
   1 teaspoon salt
   $1/4$ teaspoon pepper
   2 medium stalks celery, chopped (about
      1 cup)
   1 medium onion, chopped (about $1/2$ cup)
   4 hard-cooked eggs, chopped

Heat 1 inch salted water ($1/4$ teaspoon salt, if desired, to 1 cup water) to boiling; add potatoes. Cover and heat to boiling; reduce heat. Cook 30 to 35 minutes or until potatoes are tender; drain. Cool slightly; cut into cubes (about 6 cups).

Mix mayonnaise, vinegar, mustard, salt and pepper in 4-quart glass or plastic bowl. Add potatoes, celery and onion; toss. Stir in eggs. Cover and refrigerate at least 4 hours.   **10 servings**

SERVING SIZE: 1 Serving 340 Calories (250 Calories from Fat); Fat 28 g (Saturated 5 g); Cholesterol 105 mg; Sodium 460 mg; Carbohydrate 19 g; (Dietary Fiber 1 g); Protein 4 g; *% Daily Value:* Vitamin A 4%; Vitamin C 6%; Calcium 2%; Iron 4%

Garden Potato Salad

Ordinary potato salad weighs in at about three times the calories of this version, crunchy with added vegetables.

1 cup plain nonfat yogurt
1 tablespoon reduced-calorie French dressing
2 teaspoons prepared mustard
1/2 teaspoon celery seed
1/2 teaspoon salt
1/4 teaspoon pepper
2 cups diced cooked potatoes
1 cup sliced radishes
1 cup diced zucchini (about 1 medium)
1 cup thinly sliced celery (about 2 medium stalks)
1/2 cup shredded carrots (about 2 medium)
1/2 cup sliced green onions (with tops)
2 hard-cooked eggs, chopped

Mix yogurt, French dressing, mustard, celery seed, salt and pepper in medium glass or plastic bowl or in heavy plastic bag. Add remaining ingredients; toss until vegetables are evenly coated. Cover and refrigerate at least 3 hours.

12 servings, about 1/2 cup each

SERVING SIZE: 1 Serving 55 Calories (10 Calories from Fat); Fat 1 g (Saturated 0 g); Cholesterol 35 mg; Sodium 150 mg; Carbohydrate 9 g; (Dietary Fiber 1 g); Protein 3 g; *% Daily Value:* Vitamin A 8%; Vitamin C 6%; Calcium 6%; Iron 2%

French Potato Salad

6 medium potatoes (about 2 pounds)
1/4 teaspoon instant beef or chicken bouillon
1/3 cup hot water
1/3 cup dry white wine or chicken broth
Tarragon Dressing (below)
3 tablespoons snipped parsley

Heat 1 inch salted water (1/2 teaspoon salt to 1 cup water) to boiling. Add potatoes. Heat to boiling; reduce heat. Cover and cook until tender, 30 to 35 minutes; drain and cool.

Cut potatoes into 1/4-inch slices. Place in glass or plastic bowl. Dissolve bouillon in hot water; add wine. Pour over potatoes. Cover and refrigerate, stirring occasionally, until cold, 3 to 4 hours but no longer than 24 hours.

Drain potatoes; toss with Tarragon Dressing until coated. Sprinkle with parsley. **4 to 6 servings**

Tarragon Dressing

3 tablespoons olive or vegetable oil
2 tablespoons tarragon wine vinegar
2 teaspoons snipped chives
1 teaspoon salt
1 teaspoon Dijon-style mustard
1/2 teaspoon dried tarragon leaves
1/8 teaspoon pepper
1 clove garlic, cut into halves

Shake all ingredients in tightly covered container; discard garlic.

SERVING SIZE: 1 Serving 240 Calories (90 Calories from Fat); Fat 10 g (Saturated 2 g); Cholesterol 0 mg; Sodium 640 mg; Carbohydrate 38 g; (Dietary Fiber 3 g); Protein 3 g; *% Daily Value:* Vitamin A 2%; Vitamin C 14%; Calcium 2%; Iron 4%

Hot German Vegetable Salad

We slimmed down the traditional hot German potato salad, but kept all the great taste!

1/2 **pound new potatoes (3 or 4), cut into fourths**
1/2 **pound turnips (2 or 3 small), peeled and cut into fourths**
2 slices bacon
1/2 **cup chopped onion (about 1 medium)**
1 tablespoon all-purpose flour
2 teaspoons sugar
1/2 **teaspoon salt**
1/4 **teaspoon celery seed**
Dash of pepper
1/2 **cup water**
1/4 **cup vinegar**
1 cup coarsely shredded cabbage

Heat 1 inch water to boiling. Add potatoes and turnips. Heat to boiling; reduce heat. Cover and cook until tender, 15 to 20 minutes; drain. Cool slightly; cut into 1/2-inch pieces.

Cook bacon in 10-inch skillet until crisp; remove bacon and drain. Cook and stir onion in bacon fat until tender. Stir in flour, sugar, salt, celery seed and pepper. Cook over low heat until onion is evenly coated, stirring constantly; remove from heat. Stir in water and vinegar. Heat to boiling, stirring constantly. Boil and stir 1 minute; remove from heat. Stir in shredded cabbage. Crumble bacon; stir bacon, potatoes and turnips into cabbage mixture. Cook until hot and bubbly, stirring gently to coat vegetables. **6 servings, about 1/2 cup each**

SERVING SIZE: 1 Serving 65 Calories (10 Calories from Fat); Fat 1 g (Saturated 0 g); Cholesterol 2 mg; Sodium 230 mg; Carbohydrate 14 g; (Dietary Fiber 2 g); Protein 2 g; *% Daily Value:* Vitamin A *%; Vitamin C 10%; Calcium 2%; Iron 4%

Sunchoke and Spinach Salad

Sunchokes, or Jerusalem artichokes, are paired with lime for a refreshing taste. When entertaining, serve on shredded lettuce, as we've suggested. For a more casual meal, toss the lettuce in with the other ingredients.

Lime-Yogurt Dressing (below)
2 cups shredded spinach
1 cup finely chopped peeled Jerusalem artichokes (about 4 medium)
1 cup shopped carrots (about 2 medium)
1/2 **cup chopped red bell pepper (about 1 small)**
1/2 **cup finely chopped red onion (about 1/2 medium)**
2 cups shredded lettuce

Prepare Lime-Yogurt Dressing in large glass or plastic bowl. Add remaining ingredients except lettuce; toss. Cover and refrigerate about 2 hours or until chilled. Serve on lettuce.

6 servings

Lime-Yogurt Dressing

3/4 **cup plain nonfat yogurt**
3 tablespoons chopped fresh parsley
2 tablespoons lime juice
2 tablespoons red wine vinegar or cider vinegar
1/2 **teaspoon grated lime peel**
1/2 **teaspoon salt**
1/4 **teaspoon pepper**

Mix all ingredients with fork or wire whisk.

SERVING SIZE: 1 Serving 65 Calories (0 Calories from Fat); Fat 0 g (Saturated 0 g); Cholesterol 0 mg; Sodium 220 mg; Carbohydrate 13 g; (Dietary Fiber 2 g); Protein 3 g; *% Daily Value:* Vitamin A 44%; Vitamin C 48%; Calcium 8%; Iron 4%

Sunchoke and Spinach Salad

Spinach with Sprouts

8 ounces fresh spinach or curly endive
Sesame Dressing (below)
1 can (16 ounces) bean sprouts*, rinsed
**   and drained**
1 can (8¹/₂ ounces) water chestnuts,
**   drained and sliced**
1 cup croutons

Tear spinach into bite-size pieces. Prepare Sesame Dressing. Add bean sprouts, water chestnuts and dressing; toss. Sprinkle with croutons.   **8 servings, about ³/₄ cup each**

*2 cups fresh sprouts can be substituted for the canned bean sprouts.

Sesame Dressing

¹/₄ cup soy sauce
2 tablespoons toasted sesame seeds
2 tablespoons lemon juice
1 tablespoon finely chopped onion
¹/₂ teaspoon sugar
¹/₄ teaspoon pepper

Shake all ingredients in tightly covered container.

SERVING SIZE: 1 Serving 130 Calories (45 Calories from Fat); Fat 5 g (Saturated 1 g); Cholesterol 0 mg; Sodium 570 mg; Carbohydrate 15 g; (Dietary Fiber 3 g); Protein 9 g; *% Daily Value:* Vitamin A 16%; Vitamin C 26%; Calcium 6%; Iron 12%

Blue Cheese Waldorf Salad

Blue Cheese Dressing (right)
2 medium unpeeled red eating apples, cut
**   into ¹/₄-inch slices**
Lemon juice
Spinach leaves
¹/₂ cup thinly sliced celery (about
**   1 medium stalk)**
2 tablespoons chopped toasted walnuts

Prepare Blue Cheese Dressing. Sprinkle apple slices with lemon juice. Arrange apple slices on spinach leaves. Spoon Blue Cheese Dressing over salad; sprinkle with celery and walnuts.

4 servings

Blue Cheese Dressing

¹/₃ cup plain nonfat yogurt
1 tablespoon reduced-calorie mayonnaise
**   or salad dressing**
1 tablespoon finely crumbled blue cheese

Mix all ingredients; cover and refrigerate at least 1 hour.

SERVING SIZE: 1 Serving 95 Calories (35 Calories from Fat); Fat 4 g (Saturated 1 g); Cholesterol 5 mg; Sodium 90 mg; Carbohydrate 14 g; (Dietary Fiber 2 g); Protein 3 g; *% Daily Value:* Vitamin A 8%; Vitamin C 14%; Calcium 8%; Iron 2%

Wilted Mixed Green Salad

8 cups bite-size pieces salad greens
**   (spinach, red leaf lettuce, Boston**
**   lettuce, romaine)**
¹/₄ cup white or cider vinegar
2 teaspoons sugar
¹/₂ teaspoon salt
1¹/₂ teaspoons snipped fresh or ¹/₂ teaspoon
**   dried dill weed**
¹/₂ teaspoon dry mustard
Dash of pepper
2 tablespoons water
1 tablespoon vegetable oil
2 slices bacon, crisply cooked and
**   crumbled**

Place greens in salad bowl. Heat remaining ingredients except bacon to boiling. Pour over greens and toss. Sprinkle with bacon.

8 servings

SERVING SIZE: 1 Serving 45 Calories (25 Calories from Fat); Fat 3 g (Saturated 1 g); Cholesterol 0 mg; Sodium 165 mg; Carbohydrate 3 g; (Dietary Fiber 0 g); Protein 1 g; *% Daily Value:* Vitamin A 2%; Vitamin C 2%; Calcium *%; Iron 2%

Spinach Salad

Chopped egg and crumbled bacon are added to fresh, tender spinach leaves for flavor and color.

1 clove garlic, slivered
¹/₃ cup vegetable oil
¹/₄ cup wine vinegar
¹/₄ teaspoon salt
Dash of pepper
12 ounces spinach, torn into bite-size pieces
1 hard-cooked egg, chopped
2 slices bacon, crisply cooked and crumbled

Let garlic stand in oil 1 hour; discard garlic. Mix oil, vinegar, salt and pepper in salad bowl. Add spinach; toss until leaves are well coated. Sprinkle with egg and bacon; toss.   **3 servings**

SERVING SIZE: 1 Serving 290 Calories (250 Calories from Fat); Fat 28 g (Saturated 5 g); Cholesterol 75 mg; Sodium 330 mg; Carbohydrate 5 g; (Dietary Fiber 2 g); Protein 6 g; *% Daily Value:* Vitamin A 70%; Vitamin C 40%; Calcium 8%; Iron 14%

Mushroom and Fennel Salad

¹/₄ cup olive or vegetable oil
2 tablespoons white wine vinegar
¹/₂ teaspoon salt
¹/₈ teaspoon dried dill weed
2 large cloves garlic, crushed
2 cups thinly sliced fennel bulb
3 cups sliced mushrooms (about 8 ounces)
¹/₄ cup sliced green onions (with tops)
Bibb lettuce leaves

Shake oil, vinegar, salt, dill weed and garlic in tightly covered container. Pour over fennel, mushrooms and green onions; toss until evenly coated. Cover and refrigerate at least 2 hours. Serve on lettuce leaves. Sprinkle with freshly ground pepper, if desired.

SERVING SIZE: 1 Serving 100 Calories (80 Calories from Fat); Fat 9 g (Saturated 1 g); Cholesterol 0 mg; Sodium 200 mg; Carbohydrate 5 g; (Dietary Fiber 1 g); Protein 1 g; *% Daily Value:* Vitamin A *%; Vitamin C 10%; Calcium 2%; Iron 4%

Coleslaw

¹/₂ cup sour cream or plain yogurt
¹/₄ cup mayonnaise or salad dressing
1 teaspoon sugar
¹/₂ teaspoon dry mustard
¹/₂ teaspoon seasoned salt
¹/₈ teaspoon pepper
¹/₂ medium head cabbage, finely shredded or chopped (about 4 cups)
1 medium carrot, shredded (about ¹/₂ cup)
1 small onion, chopped (about ¹/₄ cup)

Mix sour cream, mayonnaise, sugar, mustard, seasoned salt and pepper. Toss with cabbage, carrot and onion. Sprinkle with paprika or dill weed, if desired.   **8 servings, about ¹/₂ cup each**

SERVING SIZE: 1 Serving 95 Calories (70 Calories from Fat); Fat 8 g (Saturated 3 g); Cholesterol 15 mg; Sodium 145 mg; Carbohydrate 6 g; (Dietary Fiber 1 g); Protein 1 g; *% Daily Value:* Vitamin A 16%; Vitamin C 32%; Calcium 4%; Iron 2%

Heartland Three-Bean Salad

Not everyone agrees on which 3 beans to include in this hearty salad. You can count on finding green beans and wax beans in most recipes; and while many recipes— including ours—use kidney beans, some call for lima beans instead. Of course, you can add lima beans to this recipe and enjoy a 4-bean salad!

1 can (16 ounces) cut green beans, drained
1 can (16 ounces) cut wax beans, drained
1 can (15 ounces) kidney beans, drained
1 cup thinly sliced onion rings, cut in half
1 small bell pepper, finely chopped (about ¹/₂ cup)
2 tablespoons chopped fresh parsley
²/₃ cup vinegar
¹/₂ cup sugar
¹/₃ cup vegetable oil
¹/₂ teaspoon pepper
¹/₂ teaspoon salt
2 slices bacon, crisply cooked and crumbled

Mix beans onion, bell pepper and parsley in 3-quart bowl. Mix remaining ingredients in 1¹/₂-quart saucepan. Heat vinegar mixture to boiling, stirring occasionally. Pour over beans; stir. Cover and refrigerate, stirring occasionally, at least 3 hours or until chilled. Just before serving, sprinkle with bacon. **12 servings**

SERVING SIZE: 1 Serving 135 Calories (65 Calories from Fat); Fat 7 g (Saturated 1 g); Cholesterol 1 mg; Sodium 420 mg; Carbohydrate 19 g; (Dietary Fiber 4 g); Protein 3 g; *% Daily Value:* Vitamin A 4%; Vitamin C 22%; Calcium 2%; Iron 8%

Parmesan-Basil Vegetables

These zesty vegetables are great to make ahead and then serve with grilled chicken or fish.

¹/₃ cup grated Parmesan cheese
²/₃ cup mayonnaise, salad dressing or plain yogurt
2 tablespoons vinegar
1 tablespoon chopped fresh or 1 teaspoon dried basil leaves
1 clove garlic, finely chopped
2 cups bite-size pieces broccoli flowerets and stems
1¹/₂ cups cauliflowerets
1 medium zucchini, cut into cubes
1 medium carrot, thinly sliced
1 small onion, thinly sliced and separated into rings

Mix cheese, mayonnaise, vinegar, basil and garlic in large glass or plastic bowl. Stir in remaining ingredients. Cover and refrigerate at least 2 hours. **6 servings, about 1 cup each**

SERVING SIZE: 1 Serving 225 Calories (190 Calories from Fat); Fat 21 g (Saturated 4 g); Cholesterol 20 mg; Sodium 240 mg; Carbohydrate 7 g; (Dietary Fiber 2 g); Protein 4 g; *% Daily Value:* Vitamin A 26%; Vitamin C 72%; Calcium 10%; Iron 4%

Cauliflower and Avocado Salad

**1 medium head cauliflower (about
    2 pounds), separated into flowerets
2 tablespoons vinegar
2 tablespoons vegetable oil
¹/₂ teaspoon salt
Dash of pepper
Southwest Guacamole (below)
Romaine
2 tablespoons slivered almonds**

Heat 1 inch water to boiling. Add cauliflower. Cover and heat to boiling; reduce heat. Boil 4 minutes; drain. Immediately rinse under cold running water; drain.

Mix vinegar and oil in large glass or plastic bowl. Add cauliflower, salt and pepper; toss. Cover and refrigerate at least 1 hour. Prepare Southwest Guacamole.

Just before serving, arrange cauliflower on romaine; top with Southwest Guacamole. Sprinkle with almonds.   **6 to 8 servings**

Southwest Guacamole

**5 ripe avocados, peeled and pitted
4 cloves garlic, finely chopped
1 medium tomato, chopped (about 1 cup)
¹/₄ cup lime juice
¹/₂ teaspoon salt**

Mash avocados in a medium bowl until slightly lumpy. Stir in remaining ingredients. Cover and refrigerate 1 hour.

SERVING SIZE: 1 Serving 200 Calories (155 Calories from Fat); Fat 17 g (Saturated 3 g); Cholesterol 0 mg; Sodium 310 mg; Carbohydrate 13 g; (Dietary Fiber 5 g); Protein 4 g; *% Daily Value:* Vitamin A 8%; Vitamin C 46%; Calcium 4%; Iron 8%

Head Start Salad Dressings

For Fruit Salads: Take full advantage of prepared dressings but give them a hint of "homemade." You can add that personal touch with any of the following combinations.

- ¹/₄ cup of chunky blue cheese salad dressing and 1 tablespoon apricot preserves
- ¹/₄ cup of chunky blue cheese salad dressing and 2 tablespoons French salad dressing
- ¹/₄ cup of chunky blue cheese salad dressing and ¹/₈ teaspoon curry powder
- ¹/₄ cup of fruit salad dressing and ¹/₄ teaspoon sesame seed
- ¹/₄ cup French salad dressing and ¹/₈ teaspoon celery seed
- ¹/₂ cup mayonnaise or salad dressing, 2 tablespoons cranberry juice cocktail and ¹/₄ teaspoon poppy seed

Ambrosia Fruit Salad

Although myriad variations exist, this heavenly salad or dessert always contains oranges and coconut. It is best served icy cold. Ambrosia was the food of the Greek gods.

1 large grapefruit, peeled and sectioned
3 medium oranges, peeled and sectioned
¹/₂ cup seedless green grape halves
1 to 2 tablespoons light corn syrup
1 tablespoon dry sherry, if desired
1 large banana, sliced
¹/₄ cup flaked coconut

Cut grapefruit sections into halves. Mix grapefruit, oranges, grapes, corn syrup and sherry. Cover and refrigerate at least 2 hours but no longer than 24 hours. Stir in banana and coconut just before serving. **6 servings**

SERVING SIZE: 1 Serving 100 Calories (10 Calories from Fat); Fat 1 g (Saturated 1 g); Cholesterol 0 mg; Sodium 15 mg; Carbohydrate 25 g; (Dietary Fiber 3 g); Protein 1 g; *% Daily Value:* Vitamin A 2%; Vitamin C 100%; Calcium 4%; Iron 2%

Melon Salad with Tea-flavored Cream

Tea adds a gently mysterious flavor to the topping. Most people wouldn't be able to identify it as tea—they just like it.

1 cup boiling water
1 package (0.3 ounce) sugar-free orange-flavored gelatin
³/₄ cup unsweetened orange juice
¹/₄ teaspoon ground ginger
2 cups small cantaloupe or honeydew balls
Tea-flavored Cream (right)

Pour boiling water on gelatin in medium bowl; stir until gelatin is dissolved. Stir in orange juice and ginger. Refrigerate until slightly thickened but not set.

Stir in melon balls. Pour into a 4-cup mold or 6 individual molds. Refrigerate until firm, at least 4 hours; unmold. Spoon about 1 tablespoon Tea-flavored Cream onto each serving. **6 servings, about ²/₃ cup with 1 tablespoon topping each**

Tea-flavored Cream

¹/₂ cup frozen (thawed) whipped topping
1 teaspoon instant unsweetened tea (dry)

Mix ingredients.

SERVING SIZE: 1 Serving 60 Calories (20 Calories from Fat); Fat 2 g (Saturated 1 g); Cholesterol 0 mg; Sodium 35 mg; Carbohydrate 10 g; (Dietary Fiber 0 g); Protein 1 g; *% Daily Value:* Vitamin A 14%; Vitamin C 58%; Calcium *%; Iron *%

Cranberry-Raspberry Salad

2 packages (12 ounces each) cranberry-orange sauce
1 package (12 ounces) cranberry-raspberry sauce
1 package (6 ounces) lemon gelatin
2 cups boiling water

Lightly oil 6¹/₂-cup ring mold. Mix cranberry sauces together in large bowl. Dissolve gelatin in boiling water; stir into cranberry sauces. Pour into mold. Cover and refrigerate overnight.

Unmold salad. Garnish with watercress and cranberries, if desired. **10 servings**

SERVING SIZE: 1 Serving 165 Calories (0 Calories from Fat); Fat 0 g (Saturated 0 g); Cholesterol 0 mg; Sodium 35 mg; Carbohydrate 42 g; (Dietary Fiber 1 g); Protein 0 g; *% Daily Value:* Vitamin A *%; Vitamin C 2%; Calcium *%; Iron *%

Ambrosia Fruit Salad

Molded Salads

Salad molds: Plain or fancy, large or small, almost anything that doesn't leak can be used. The gelatin will thicken and firm more quickly in containers of thin metal, such as ice cube trays or stainless steel bowls.

Molds of unknown size: You can measure the size of these by filling with water, then measuring the water. Don't try to adjust the ingredient amount to fit odd-size molds. Pour the extra into smaller containers.

Flavored and unflavored gelatin: Follow the directions carefully since methods are different.

Salads in a hurry: Check package for quick-set directions. Or speed up thickening by placing mixture in freezer or a bowl of ice and water and removing it when it starts to thicken. (If it becomes too solid, let it soften over hot water.)

Adding solids: Before you add fruits or vegetables, let the gelatin mixture thicken to the consistency of beaten egg white. Drain solids thoroughly before adding them.

To make rainbow effect: Layer different colors of gelatin, allowing each color to set before adding the next layer.

To unmold salad: Quickly dip salad into hot water to top of mold. Loosen the edge of the salad with the tip of a paring knife. Place a plate on top of the mold and, holding tightly, invert plate and mold. Shake mold gently and remove carefully. Repeat these steps if necessary.

Rainbow Party Mold

Using frozen raspberries hastens the thickening process.

1 cup boiling water
1 package (3 ounces) lemon-flavored gelatin
³/₄ cup sparkling white grape juice, chilled
1 cup chopped fresh, frozen (thawed) or canned (drained) peaches
1¹/₂ cups boiling water
1 package (6 ounces) lime-flavored gelatin
2 cups plain or vanilla-flavored yogurt
2 cups boiling water
1 package (6 ounces) raspberry-flavored gelatin
1¹/₂ cups sparkling white grape juice, chilled
1 cup fresh or frozen raspberries

Pour 1 cup boiling water on lemon gelatin; stir until gelatin is dissolved. Stir in ³/₄ cup grape juice. Refrigerate until the consistency of unbeaten egg whites. Stir in peaches. Pour into 12-cup bundt cake pan. Refrigerate until set but not firm.

Pour 1¹/₂ cups boiling water on lime gelatin; stir until gelatin is dissolved. Stir in yogurt. Pour over lemon layer. Refrigerate until set but not firm.

Pour 2 cups boiling water on raspberry gelatin; stir until gelatin is dissolved. Stir in 1¹/₂ cups grape juice. Refrigerate until the consistency of unbeaten egg whites. Stir in raspberries. Pour over lime layer. Refrigerate about 4 hours or until firm; unmold. (Do not refrigerate longer than 48 hours.) **20 servings**

SERVING SIZE: 1 Serving 52 Calories (0 Calories from Fat); Fat 0 g (Saturated 0 g); Cholesterol 0 mg; Sodium 25 mg; Carbohydrate 11 g; (Dietary Fiber 0 g); Protein 2 g; *% Daily Value:* Vitamin A *%; Vitamin C 6%; Calcium 4%; Iron *%

Molded Tangerine Salad

1 envelope unflavored gelatin
1 cup cold water
1 can (6 ounces) frozen tangerine juice
    concentrate, thawed
1 package (8 ounces) Neufchâtel or cream
    cheese, softened
1 can (8 ounces) crushed pineapple in
    juice, well drained
Watercress
1 kiwi, sliced

Sprinkle gelatin on cold water in 1-quart saucepan to soften; heat over low heat, stirring constantly, until gelatin is dissolved. Remove from heat; stir in juice concentrate. Beat cheese in 2 1/2-quart bowl on medium speed until fluffy. Gradually beat in gelatin mixture on low speed until smooth. Refrigerate until slightly thickened, about 1 hour. Stir in pineapple. Pour into 4-cup mold. Refrigerate until firm, about 2 hours. Unmold on serving plate. Garnish with watercress and kiwi.   **6 servings, about 1/4 cup each**

SERVING SIZE: 1 Serving 190 Calories (80 Calories from Fat); Fat 9 g (Saturated 6 g); Cholesterol 30 mg; Sodium 160 mg; Carbohydrate 22 g; (Dietary Fiber 1 g); Protein 6 g; *% Daily Value:* Vitamin A 12%; Vitamin C 54%; Calcium 4%; Iron 2%

Strawberry-Kiwifruit-Spinach Salad

This pretty red and green salad makes a nice Christmas dish.

1 pint fresh strawberries, cut into halves
2 kiwifruit, peeled and sliced
1 medium bunch fresh spinach, washed
    and torn into pieces
Dressing (right)

Combine all ingredients in large bowl. Pour dressing over salad just before serving.

Dressing

1/3 cup vegetable oil
2 tablespoons strawberry vinegar
2 tablespoons strawberry jam

Combine all ingredients.

SERVING SIZE: 1 Serving 170 Calories (115 Calories from Fat); Fat 13 g (Saturated 2 g); Cholesterol 0 mg; Sodium 50 mg; Carbohydrate 14 g; (Dietary Fiber 3 g); Protein 2 g; *% Daily Value:* Vitamin A 48%; Vitamin C 100%; Calcium 6%; Iron 10%

Easy Fruit Salad

2/3 cup plain yogurt
1 tablespoon honey
1 tablespoon lemon juice
1 cup seedless grapes
1 can (11 ounces) mandarin orange
    segments
1 can (8 1/4 ounces) pineapple chunks in
    syrup
1 red apple, sliced
1 cup bite-size salad greens

Drain mandarin oranges and pineapple. Mix yogurt, honey and lemon juice in medium bowl. Stir in remaining ingredients.   **4 servings**

SERVING SIZE: 1 Serving 160 Calories (10 Calories from Fat); Fat 1 g (Saturated 1 g); Cholesterol 2 mg; Sodium 35 mg; Carbohydrate 37 g; (Dietary Fiber 2 g); Protein 3 g; *% Daily Value:* Vitamin A 2%; Vitamin C 42%; Calcium 10%; Iron 4%

METRIC CONVERSION GUIDE

U.S. UNITS	CANADIAN METRIC	AUSTRALIAN METRIC
Volume		
1/4 teaspoon	1 mL	1 ml
1/2 teaspoon	2 mL	2 ml
1 teaspoon	5 mL	5 ml
1 tablespoon	15 mL	20 ml
1/4 cup	50 mL	60 ml
1/3 cup	75 mL	80 ml
1/2 cup	125 mL	125 ml
2/3 cup	150 mL	170 ml
3/4 cup	175 mL	190 ml
1 cup	250 mL	250 ml
1 quart	1 liter	1 liter
1 1/2 quarts	1.5 liter	1.5 liter
2 quarts	2 liters	2 liters
2 1/2 quarts	2.5 liters	2.5 liters
3 quarts	3 liters	3 liters
4 quarts	4 liters	4 liters
Weight		
1 ounce	30 grams	30 grams
2 ounces	55 grams	60 grams
3 ounces	85 grams	90 grams
4 ounces (1/4 pound)	115 grams	125 grams
8 ounces (1/2 pound)	225 grams	225 grams
16 ounces (1 pound)	455 grams	500 grams
1 pound	455 grams	1/2 kilogram

Measurements		**Temperatures**	
Inches	Centimeters	Fahrenheit	Celsius
1	2.5	32°	0°
2	5.0	212°	100°
3	7.5	250°	120°
4	10.0	275°	140°
5	12.5	300°	150°
6	15.0	325°	160°
7	17.5	350°	180°
8	20.5	375°	190°
9	23.0	400°	200°
10	25.5	425°	220°
11	28.0	450°	230°
12	30.5	475°	240°
13	33.0	500°	260°
14	35.5		
15	38.0		

NOTE
The recipes in this cookbook have not been developed or tested using metric measures. When converting recipes to metric, some variations in quality may be noted.

Index

Page numbers in *italics* indicate photographs.